Alger Hiss and the Battle for History

Alger Hiss

Battle f

YALE UNIVERSITY PRESS   NEW HAVEN & LONDON

AND THE

r History

Susan Jacoby

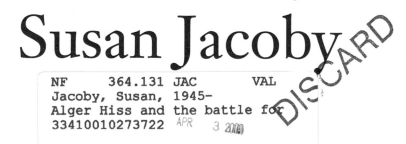

Published with assistance from the Kingsley Trust Association Publication
Fund established by the Scroll and Key Society of Yale College.

Set in Janson type by Integrated Publishing Solutions.
Printed in the United States of America.

Library of Congress Cataloging-in-Publication Data

Jacoby, Susan, 1945–
Alger Hiss and the battle for history / Susan Jacoby.
p.   cm.—(Icons of America)
Includes bibliographical references and index.
ISBN 978-0-300-12133-9 (cloth : alk. paper)
1. Hiss, Alger.   2. Communism—United States—History—20th
century.   3. Espionage, Soviet—United States—History—20th century.
4. United States. Dept. of State—Officials and Employees—Biography.
5. United States. Congress. House. Committee on Un-American Activities.
6. Cold War.   7. United States—Politics and government—1945–1989.
8. United States—Politics and government—1989–.   9. Political culture—
United States.   10. Right and left (Political science)   I. Title.
E743.5.H55J33 2009
364.1′31—dc22
[B]

2008036177

A catalogue record for this book is available from the British Library.

This paper meets the requirements of ANSI/NISO Z39.48-1992
(Permanence of Paper).
It contains 30 percent postconsumer waste (PCW) and is certified by the
Forest Stewardship Council (FSC).

10 9 8 7 6 5 4 3 2 1

In memory of Alfred G. Meyer

Contents

Contents

Alger Hiss and the Battle for History

Introduction

As a child in the 1950s, I first heard about the Alger Hiss case because my father was an accountant with the unprofessional habit of writing down important figures on scraps of paper and promptly losing them. "Bob, go out and look for them in some pumpkin patch," my mother would invariably say, as Dad searched futilely for the errant papers around the house. Understandably bewildered by what the adults considered a joke, I asked what my father's missing papers had to do with pumpkins and was treated to a brief synopsis of the 1948 House Committee on Un-American Activities hearings, featuring the dueling testimonies of Hiss and Whittaker Chambers. The story was somewhat confusing to me: it seemed that this man Chambers had accused Hiss of having been some sort of Communist spy while working for the government, and Hiss had gone to jail not for spying but for lying about having been Chambers's friend. . . . My parents (like many other Americans, I suspect) did not have the details straight themselves. They told me that Hiss was the one who had hidden confidential government documents in a pumpkin. In fact, Chambers was the one who had used a hollowed-out gourd to hide the microfilm, which he said he had received from Hiss. When Chambers finally did turn over the goods to congressional investigators, he led them on a nighttime search for the correct pumpkin in his backyard. As described in hilarious detail by his biographer Sam Tanenhaus, Chambers apparently fumbled around with several intact pumpkins before he found the one he had scooped out in order to create a secure hiding place.[1] At the time, no one could have imagined that the Chambers farm, including the sacred ground that was once the pumpkin patch, would one day be declared a national historic landmark by President Ronald Reagan.

My parents, despite their confusion about who did what to the pumpkin, told me they were certain that Hiss deserved to go to jail but that Chambers was also a liar. I tell this story only to illustrate the degree to which the competing narratives of Hiss and Chambers were embedded, however imprecisely, in popular consciousness at the height of the Cold War era. My parents were politically aware but not politically obsessed; they had voted—again, like the majority of Americans—for both Franklin D. Roosevelt and Dwight D. Eisenhower. They were completely removed from the intellectual and activist political circles in which belief in the guilt or innocence of Hiss was a litmus test of personal and social loyalty. They worried about the possibility of nuclear war more than they worried about communists. They disliked Senator Joseph R. McCarthy and despised Richard Nixon—not because of his role in the Hiss case but because they saw him (and would continue to see him for the rest of his political career) as Tricky Dick. Indeed, they could not figure out why a man with as sunny a public persona as Eisenhower would choose to be linked with the dour Nixon, who, as my dad remarked, always reminded him of the character in *L'il Abner*, Joe Btfsplk, who walked around with a rain cloud constantly hovering above his head. My parents were thoroughgoing moderates, in today's political parlance, and they were largely indifferent to what Alistair Cooke, then the Washington correspondent of the *Manchester Guardian*, described as an atmosphere "something very like a seventeenth-century religious war, when the outside pressure to swallow whole the Hiss story or the Chambers story, and to join one or other of the entailed crusades, was almost irresistible."[2] In *A Generation on Trial* (1950), the best and the only reasonably objective contemporary account of the Hiss case, Cooke also predicted that the affair would "offer for some time to come, and perhaps forever, as many puzzles as the celebrated Wallace case (the Liverpool chess-player, not the Iowa politician)." *

When I told my eighty-six-year-old mother that I was writing a book about changing public perceptions of the Hiss case, she sent me an e-mail asking in a bewildered tone, "Who cares about that anymore?" When I explained to her that a great many intellectuals and political activists still cared deeply and that I had just attended a conference at New York University of several hundred people who continue to believe that Hiss was framed by a right-wing conspiracy, she replied shrewdly, "I'll bet there weren't too many people under seventy at that con-

---

*William Wallace, a Liverpool insurance agent and amateur chess player, was convicted of bludgeoning his wife, Julia, to death in a case as famous in the 1930s as the O. J. Simpson case would become sixty years later. The verdict was overturned on appeal, but the real killer—if indeed Wallace was innocent—was never found. The other Wallace—Iowa-born Henry—was FDR's vice president from 1940 to 1944 and the 1948 Progressive Party presidential candidate.

ference." She advised me that any book about Hiss would have to tell people in their thirties, forties, and fifties why, with the Soviet Union long gone and stateless terrorism the major threat to American security, they should care about this old chapter in the Cold War.

The relatively swift (as imperial epochs go) collapse of Soviet Communism should logically have taken nearly all of the heat out of emblematic Cold War controversies, including the Hiss case and the executions of Julius and Ethel Rosenberg. Hiss, in particular, seems at first glance to have been an unlikely candidate for the leading role in a long-term cause célèbre. Unlike the Rosenbergs, he was charged not with spying but only with perjury. His penalty was not death but forty-four months in a federal prison. Most of his life after jail—especially after 1970—was spent in relatively comfortable circumstances, which included the restoration of his federal pension and his right to practice law; numerous speaking engagements; and the undying loyalty of many who continued to believe that he had been framed and was a victim of Cold War hysteria and right-wing hostility toward the New Deal.

The sequence of the events in the case, unlike the political interpretation, is fairly straightforward. In the summer of 1948, Chambers, an editor at *Time* magazine and a former member of the American Communist Party who had become a rabid anti-Communist, took the stand before the House Committee on Un-American Activities Committee (HUAC) to tell a story about Alger Hiss, a former rising star in the State Department who was by then the president of the prestigious Carnegie Endowment for International Peace.* The story Chambers told was that he and Hiss had been friends and fellow Communists in the 1930s—that Hiss was, in fact, his best friend in the Party. At first Chambers denied that he and Hiss had engaged in espionage, but a few months later (after the statute of limitations on espionage had expired), he led HUAC investigators to the microfilm concealed in the famous hollowed-out pumpkin on his Maryland farm. "What is this, Dick Tracy?" asked one of the FBI investigators, who bemusedly watched Chambers fumble around in the dark before he found the right pumpkin.[3]

Hiss, who had at first denied knowing Chambers at all, admitted that he had known him under another name but denied having been a member of the Communist Party or having handed over any government documents. Hiss's most aggressive questioner at the HUAC hearings was

---

*Although the acronym for the House Committee should, technically, be HCUA, I bow to the euphony of HUAC, which has been used in most newspapers, magazines, and books for the past sixty years.

Nixon, a previously obscure young congressman from California. Nixon, who for some time had been promising his wife, Pat, a second honeymoon (or at least a vacation), decamped from what was supposed to be a relaxing, romantic cruise through the Panama Canal after he was informed about the discovery of the pumpkin papers. When Nixon received a cable from HUAC's chief investigator declaring, "Second bombshell obtained by subpoena. Case clinched," the already long-suffering Pat threw up her hands and said, "Here we go again!"[4]

During the hearings, it became clear that Hiss had known Chambers, under whatever name, reasonably well—although Chambers claimed that Hiss was his best friend in the Party and Hiss asserted that Chambers was a mere acquaintance, known to him only as a freelance journalist named George Crosley and as a deadbeat who failed to pay back small loans. Hiss never explained exactly why he would lend money, in the depths of the Depression, to someone who was only an acquaintance. After the hearings, Hiss was indicted and tried twice for perjury, while Chambers—who admitted to having perjured himself about his own past as a spy—was never prosecuted. Hiss's first trial ended in a hung jury in July 1949. The second trial, which began in November 1949, resulted in Hiss's conviction. Between the first and the second trials, American public opinion turned more decisively against communism in general, and the Soviet Union in particular, as a result of three events. First, President Truman signed the NATO treaty and called for $1.5 billion in aid—on top of the existing Marshall Plan—to shore up Western European democracies with strong internal communist movements. Second, the U.S. State Department acknowledged that Mao Zedong's Communist Party had gained control of the Chinese mainland; this acknowledgment was followed by bitter accusations that we had "lost" China because of subversion from within the State Department. Finally, just two months before the start of the second Hiss trial, the Soviets stunned America by their first successful test explosion of an atomic bomb. It was unthinkable to the average American that the primitive Soviets, who had been saved from starvation during the war by our generous shipments of Spam (and whose heroics in stopping the German advance at Kursk and Stalingrad had already been largely forgotten by the American public), could have figured out how to make an atomic bomb on their own.*

---

*As it turned out, the Soviets *did* have a professionally trained spy (as distinct from amateurs) within the Manhattan Project. George Koval was the Iowa-born son of Jewish Communists who, in 1932, had emigrated to Birobidzhan, a region in Siberia that Stalin had designated as a "homeland" for Soviet Jews. Koval was nineteen when his family left for the Soviet Union and of

During Hiss's second trial, which began in November, HUAC was doing its part to feed public paranoia by providing a forum for witnesses who accused FDR's most trusted aide, Harry Hopkins, of having facilitated the transmission of atomic secrets to the Russians during the war. The difference between the climate of public opinion during the first and second trials may be inferred from the fact that half of the jurors questioned before the first trial were dismissed because they admitted to being prejudiced against the testimony of ex-Communists, like Chambers, who had turned into accusers of their former comrades. At the second trial's voir dire, only one potential juror said he was inclined to doubt the testimony of an ex-Communist–turned–informer.[5] On January 21, 1950, Hiss was found guilty on both counts of perjury. Until the

---

course spoke perfect, idiomatic American English. He was trained as a mole by the Soviet military intelligence agency, the GRU. After returning to the United States, Koval was drafted during World War II and sent to City College of New York by the army for training in electrical engineering. He was then hired by the Manhattan Project, where he had access to classified scientific information about the making of the atomic bomb. The FBI, it seems, had known about Koval, who eventually wound up back in the USSR, since the 1950s but never revealed the secret because it was too embarrassing to the U.S. intelligence community. On November 2, 2007, Russian President Vladimir Putin, in a move that puffed up Russian national pride while pointing out the ineptitude of American wartime security, posthumously made Dr. Koval a Hero of the Russian Federation, the highest honor that can be bestowed on a Russian citizen. One may safely assume that the skills of a spy trained by the GRU bore about the same relationship to those of Chambers, Hiss, or Rosenberg as those of Arturo Toscanani bore to a high school orchestra conductor.

end of his life he would maintain his innocence—of the formal charge of perjury and of the real charge of espionage that could no longer be made because the statute of limitations had expired.

It is extraordinary that Hiss's fate continues to generate controversy even though American communism, in both a practical and an intellectual sense, ceased to exist a half-century ago as anything other than a bogeyman for the right and a delusion for the extreme left. From the 1950s through early 1970s, liberals convinced that Hiss was framed made a number of malapropos comparisons between the Hiss and Dreyfus cases. Such comparisons are embarrassing not only, or even primarily, because the evidence against Hiss looks much stronger today as a result of what scholars have learned from American files about the case, released under the Freedom of Information Act, and from Russian and American espionage documents made accessible during the post-Soviet era. The comparisons should have been equally embarrassing in the fifties and sixties, because even if Hiss had ultimately been proved as innocent as Dreyfus, there was no comparison between the near-medieval conditions of Dreyfus's incarceration and Hiss's relatively comfortable four-year jail term, which included considerable access to newspapers, books, and letters from the outside world. But the

Hiss and Dreyfus cases are comparable in two important respects—the passion they inspired and their longevity as markers of profound political divisions within their respective nations. In view of the real and urgent issues surrounding current American intelligence capabilities, for example, it is somewhat astonishing to recall that President Bill Clinton's 1997 nomination of Anthony Lake for the directorship of the Central Intelligence Agency was derailed, at least in part, because he had said on *Meet the Press* that he was not totally sure of Hiss's guilt. As far as the political right was concerned, Lake might as well have said that the sun revolved around the earth.

One obvious factor that gives the story of Alger Hiss—or, rather, the story of how Hiss is viewed by contending factions—its iconic status is the case's position, symbolically and in real time, at the beginning of the McCarthy era. There had of course been considerable publicity surrounding the 1947 HUAC hearings aimed at the identification of Communists, ex-Communists, and fellow travelers in the motion picture industry, but pinko screenwriters were hardly in the same league, as far as either the public or politicians were concerned, as an accused traitor in the State Department. Just two weeks after Hiss was sentenced to prison for perjury, McCarthy made his famous "I have here in my hand" speech, charging extensive Communist infiltration of the State Department. Despite the passage of time and the collapse of Soviet Communism, there are few more revealing indicators of any American's overall politics than his or her assessment of McCarthyism, and this generalization applies just as strongly to Americans who came of age after the end of the McCarthy era as it does to their elders. Ask anyone what he or she thinks of HUAC or McCarthy and their effect on civil liberties in the years after the Second World War, and you don't need to ask where he or she stands on the Patriot Act today.

In *The Secret World of American Communism* (1995), Harvey Klehr, John Haynes, and Fridrikh Firsov make a careful distinction between McCarthyism and what they describe as legitimate efforts to protect government secrets from Communist espionage. Yet that distinction has almost never been maintained in real American political life. McCarthyism *was* an attack on New Deal liberalism as well as communism, and the fact that Hiss was a New Dealer—he came to Washington to work for the Agricultural Adjustment Administration in 1933—was tailor-made for those who wished to besmirch the memory of

Roosevelt. Anticommunism was an integral part of the effort to denigrate the New Deal at a time when the majority of Americans revered the memory of FDR not only as a wartime leader but as the president who gave them hope during the darkest days of the Depression. The Red-hunters made the fundamental claim that treachery by American Communist agents and fellow travelers, not the realpolitik dictated by the position of Soviet and American forces on the ground in Europe in 1945, was responsible for the emergence of the Soviet Union as a major power after the Second World War. The logical extension of that claim was a blurring of the distinction between communism and liberalism, since many of the most influential anti-Communist liberals, such as George Kennan and Arthur Schlesinger, Jr., were not only willing to credit the Soviets for their role in defeating Hitler but felt that containment and coexistence—however strained the latter might sometimes be by the former—must form the basis for an American foreign policy that would eventually thwart Soviet ambitions.

The political right, then and now, has always attempted to conflate communism (spelled with either a capital C or a lower-case c), socialism, and liberalism in domestic as well as foreign policy. If Hiss was a lying Communist Party member taking orders from the Kremlin as well as a

State Department aide at the Yalta Conference, he could be and was used as Exhibit A in support of the long-held right-wing contention that if you scratched a New Deal liberal, you might just as easily find a socialist or a communist. In domestic politics over the next twenty-five years, the conflation of communism and liberalism would take many new forms. The attempt to tar the civil rights movement of the 1960s with the communist label-libel was the first, but hardly the last, post-McCarthy example of the persistence of efforts to equate all liberal politics and dissident movements with alien, anti-American ideologies. In 1994 Newt Gingrich, the architect of the historic Republican takeover of both houses of Congress during Clinton's first term, declared that the best way to beat the Democrats was to portray them as supporters of "Stalinist" policies and political values. That Joseph Stalin had been dead for more than forty years, and that the Soviet Union itself had ceased to exist, did not dissuade the Republican right from its conviction that Stalinism and communism could still be hot-button issues for the American electorate.*

*Ironically, it was the Republican congressional majority, led by Gingrich, that offended American bourgeois values by shutting down a great many government offices in a budget fight at the end of 1995. Seniors worrying about whether they would receive their Social Security checks on time were not amused, nor were hundreds of thousands of parents who had planned on using part of Christmas vacation to take their children to visit suddenly closed federal

The right-wing eagerness to conflate liberalism and communism made it extremely difficult for committed liberals (including some who were and are strongly anti-Communist), to separate Hiss's guilt or innocence from the more general violations of civil liberties that occurred during the McCarthy era. For many on the left, Hiss's fate has long been equated with all of the other lives broken not as punishment for espionage but simply because of past membership in a legal but highly unpopular political party (or because of association, witting or unwitting, with those who were Communist Party members). The evidence that Hiss lied does not, for liberals, eradicate the stench of injustice that wafts from so many proceedings of the period. Moreover, that stench has always been intensified by the liberal detestation of Nixon, who would certainly not have been considered a suitable running mate for Eisenhower without the national prominence he achieved as a result of the HUAC hearings. As the historian Allen Weinstein shrewdly observed after Nixon was driven from office by the Watergate scandal, nothing did more in the 1970s "to legitimize public support for Alger Hiss than the disgrace and downfall of

---

landmarks and museums like the Smithsonian Institution. Keeping the government running, it seemed, was not considered Stalinist by a majority of Americans.

Richard Nixon."[6] The reverse is also true: no one did more than Hiss to turn Nixon into a future presidential candidate.

After 1980 the deceased Chambers became as important a hero to the triumphalist New Right as he had been to the right-wingers of the 1950s. Nothing better illustrates the permanent politicization of the case than President Ronald Reagan's posthumous award to Chambers of the Medal of Freedom—a move that proved deeply offensive to many American liberals in the 1980s. It is certainly possible to be convinced of Hiss's guilt and nevertheless appalled by the bestowal of America's highest civilian honor on an informer who initially committed perjury out of fear of being prosecuted for espionage himself.

Indeed, the interest that the Hiss case still holds for the chattering and political classes cannot be understood without reference to the older split between Communists and anti-Communist liberals in the 1930s and the subsequent sub-split between anti-Communist liberals who remained liberals and those who metamorphosed into neoconservatives. The original neocons emerging from the communist and other leftist movements of the 1930s were the intellectual (and, in some instances, such as the union of Irving Kristol and Gertrude Himmelfarb, physical) parents of the current generation of powerful right-wing intellectuals in the conservative think tanks, the media, and the Republican Party. The old anti-Communist liberals who stayed liberals—such as Schlesinger, Alfred Kazin, and Irving Howe—were equally opposed to Soviet Communism and to assaults on civil liberties during the McCarthy era. Many members of the thirties' generation of anti-Communist liberals originally believed that Hiss had been framed, but nearly all of them changed their minds after the publication in 1978 of *Perjury*, the influential reexamination of the Hiss case by Weinstein (now the Archivist of the United States). The evidence against Hiss only grew stronger after the fall of the Soviet Union, when both Russian and American intelligence agencies released a great many previously classified documents, albeit in spotty and selective fashion, documenting Soviet espionage activities in the United States during the thirties, forties, and beyond. (Unfortunately, Putin, true to his values as a former KGB apparatchik, has once again cut off the flow of information from yellowing Soviet espionage files.) But there are still a handful of True Believers in Hiss on the American left. They were moved to tears by the personal testimony of Timothy Hobson, Hiss's octogenarian stepson, at the 2007 New York University conference, sponsored by the Nation Institute, titled "Alger Hiss in History." Hobson, after delivering a pained account of his inability to testify at his stepfather's trials because he was gay and his secret would have been exposed, received a standing ovation when he asserted that he *knew* Chambers had lied about being a close friend of Hiss because, as a boy, Hobson never saw Chambers around the house. Hobson's story was as painful to hear as it must have been for him to tell. Yet there was a palpable irrationality in the auditorium, where most of those attending were eager to accept a frail man's seventy-year-old memories as unimpeachable truth. I saw a pathetic spectacle of an old man trying to earn a stepfather's love from beyond the grave, while it was clear that the people sitting around me were seeing and applauding a noble defender of truth once crushed to earth. Americans of many beliefs are susceptible to blind faith.

Nearly all of the original participants in the left-wing political wars of the thirties are dead, but many passed on their political passions to their intellectual heirs. On the right, those heirs have exerted substantial political influence in every Republican administration since Reagan was elected in 1980; the middle-aged children of the old liberals-turned-neocons, based in conservative think tanks and foundations, were among the intellectual architects of the war in Iraq. The liberal intellectual heirs of both the Old Left of the thirties and the New Left of the sixties are found more commonly in academia, although they can be expected to make a governmental comeback during Democratic administrations. Bearing in mind the demise of Anthony Lake's nomination, future liberal candidates for foreign policy posts would be well advised to avoid any mention of the Hiss case.

A second factor in the persistence of the passions surrounding Hiss is the protagonist's status as an exemplar of everything the right perceived the fuzzy-headed left to be in the 1940s and, to a great extent, of everything that the political right perceives the liberal "elites" to be today. Hiss was a patrician-looking product of the best education America had to offer; a protégé of Felix Frankfurter and Oliver Wendell Holmes, Jr.; a former member of a distinguished New York law firm; a man lauded for his government service; the president of the Carnegie Endowment for International Peace—and, if Chambers was to be believed, a traitor who had worked against the interests of the society that had showered every reward on him. Conservatives were already suspicious of the United Nations, so Hiss's role as secretary general of the 1945

San Francisco organizing conference for the UN was another black mark against him. Finally, Hiss was a gentile—a not-insignificant though rarely acknowledged element in the response to his case, especially on the part of anti-Communist Jewish liberals (and Jewish conservatives, for that matter) attempting to distance themselves from the historic association between Jews and Bolshevism. Hiss's non-Jewishness would become even more important to Jewish conservatives after the Rosenbergs were convicted and executed (by which time Hiss was already in jail). In the heart of the State Department, there had been a Communist spy—and the spy was, thankfully, not only a goy but a WASP! Indeed, it is hardly surprising that not only Hiss but all of the American diplomats accused of communist sympathies were gentiles, since the prewar and wartime State Department was, to put it mildly, inhospitable to Jews.

I should say for the record that I believe Hiss was guilty of both perjury and spying, but I find evidence of the latter persuasive—very persuasive—rather than conclusive. If I were on a jury, knowing what is known now, I would certainly vote to convict Hiss. I am less convinced, however, that the information Hiss passed on was of enormous value to the Soviets (although the quality and importance of the supplied information has no bearing on whether anyone is or is not a traitor). Not even Chambers claimed that Hiss was a talented master spy. If being only 98 or 99 percent convinced of Hiss's guilt (depending on what new yet ancient "bombshell" has been released on a given day) makes me a member of the Flat Earth Society as far as the political right is concerned, so be it. As a journalist who lived and worked in Moscow from 1969 to 1972, when I met many aging survivors of the Gulag, I probably have a stronger bias than most liberals my age— I was born in 1945—against American Communists and fellow travelers who discounted reports of Stalin's crimes during the thirties. Furthermore, my firsthand experience of life in the Soviet Union also immunized me against the illusions about communism indulged in by some members of my own generation in the late sixties and early seventies. But I am not impressed by the hustlers in objective scholarly clothing who claim, "Of course, I started out believing that Hiss had been framed, but as *I actually looked at the evidence* I realized that I was wrong, that I had in fact been brainwashed by liberal orthodoxy." It has been at least twenty-five years since orthodoxy, liberal or otherwise, has maintained anything other than Hiss's guilt. The proprietors of the right-wing anti-Hiss cottage industry built and staked careers on that guilt, and many have used the dead horse to impugn the integrity of liberals like me, who view both Soviet Communism and the attack on civil liberties during the McCarthy era with deep loathing. Furthermore, my own view that Hiss lied is based less on the vast body of old and new evidence—including recently released material from Soviet and American espionage archives as well as the documents Weinstein extracted from the U.S. government in the seventies under the Freedom of Information Act—than on Hiss's own elliptical and emotionally unconvincing memoirs. Do Hiss's public recorded travels in the weeks after the Yalta Conference fit the profile of an agent named "Ales" in a decoded Soviet communication in the Venona files? Kai Bird, the Pulitzer prizewinning coauthor (with Martin J. Shermin) of *American Prometheus: The Triumph and Tragedy of J. Robert Oppenheimer* (2006), says absolutely not. Tanenhaus, author of the highly praised 1998 biography of Whittaker Chambers and now editor of the *New York Times Book Review*, calls Bird a predictable and sloppy left-wing scholar, looking for any evidence, however thin, that Hiss's conviction was unjust.[7] But even if I had never read a word of the dozens of doorstop-weight books written about the case, Hiss's slim memoir, *Recollections of a Life*, published in 1988, would have convinced me that its author was a master of what might charitably be called selective memory. My views have not been affected by the numerous testimonials, offered by his friends and his son, Tony, that the private Alger Hiss was a much warmer and more sensitive man than the cool, elusive figure who will always be known to history as the guilty protagonist of The Hiss Case. So what? Hiss's private demeanor, in spite of the many efforts to prove his guilt or innocence through bargain-basement psychology, tells us almost nothing about whether he was once a Communist with a capital C.

There is surely a disproportion in the passion that a handful of liberal intellectuals have invested in keeping open the tiny possibility that Hiss really was thoroughly innocent and was framed by the FBI. What if Hiss was the devil incarnate, and every bit as guilty as his accuser always maintained? Does that mean that liberals were wrong about the negative effects of the Cold War on American society over a long period of time? What if— and there really is no *if* about it for any clear-minded person today, in view of revelations in the 1990s from Soviet and American archives—there were some Communists in sensitive government jobs during the late 1930s and the Second World War? As a liberal, I must ask how Hiss's guilt or innocence changes anything of fundamental importance about modern American history, from the New Deal through the present era of transnational terrorism, in which fearful uncertainty has produced a near-nostalgia for the days when America's chief antagonist was a government with rulers sane enough to fear their own deaths. A conservative might well ask the same question. I believe that this nostalgia for a more predictable geopolitics also lies at the heart of the pass given for too long by prominent American conservatives to Putin, who has made great "progress" in suppressing the freedom of political speech that emerged in Russia under both Mikhail Gorbachev and Boris Yeltsin. It took Putin's 2008 invasion of Georgia to remind those still fixated on communism that aggressive Russian nationalism flourishes in the post-Soviet era.

Many analysts on both the right and the left simply assume that if Chambers was telling the truth about his and Hiss's Communist activities in the 1930s and Hiss was lying, we are required to revise our view not only of American Communism but of the geopolitical realignment that emerged from the war. There is absolutely no question, as a result of evidence in Soviet records released during the past fifteen years, that the American Communist Party was a creature of Moscow rather than the indigenous dissident political movement that inspired the fantasies of so many fellow travelers in the thirties. But what inferences, apart from the fact that the Kremlin wasted a great deal of money on its own fantasies about America, can properly be drawn from the reality of Soviet control of American Communism (if not always of individual American communists)?

Indeed, the conspicuous trait uniting Hiss's dogged ex post facto bloodhounds with his die-hard defenders is the need to be 100 percent right in order to vindicate not only their verdict on American history but the governmental policies they espouse today. The right-wing line goes something like this: liberals were wrong about Stalinism in the thirties; wrong about the influence of domestic communists; wrong about the Vietnam War; and wrong, wrong, wrong about the strength of the Soviet threat. And so it stands to reason that liberals must be wrong today in their opposition to the war in Iraq and the erosion of civil liberties associated with the war on terror. Once a naïve liberal, always a naïve liberal. On the left, the reluctance to let go of the Hiss case also has a pedigree extending from the 1930s: the right was wrong about the threat of Nazism and dismissive of the role played by Soviet Russia in holding off the Germans until America entered the war; wrong about the relative strength of American and Soviet societies after the war; wrong about the righteousness of the hunt for domestic Communists in the late forties and fifties; wrong about Vietnam; wrong about Gorbachev's sincere desire for reform; and wrong about the staying power of both communist ideology and the Soviet empire. Finally, of course, liberals believe that the right is wrong about the Iraq war and wrong in its willingness to sacrifice some of our own cherished civil liberties in order to fight terrorism. For both groups, the guilt or innocence of Alger Hiss remains today what it was in the fifties—a symbolic and real indicator of which side you were, and are, on.

American culture has always been characterized by swift eclipses of historical memory. Only three years after American and Soviet soldiers clasped hands on the banks of the Elbe River, Chambers and Hiss took center stage at the HUAC hearings—and memories of the recent wartime alliance had already been replaced by a new perception of Stalin's Soviet Union as a deadly enemy. (Today, most high school history texts still gloss over the role played by the Red Army during the Second World War. Various polls conducted during the past twenty years indicate that few Americans under forty have any idea that the Soviet Union and the United States fought on the same side.) Hiss's role in organizing the logistics for the

Yalta Conference fed directly into the postwar perception that betrayal from within, not the military realities on the ground in the closing months of the war, was responsible for the subsequent Soviet domination of Eastern Europe. Let us assume, for the sake of argument, that the "Ales" mentioned in various decoded intelligence documents was Alger Hiss and that Hiss passed on advance knowledge about American and British negotiating positions to Soviet intelligence agents before the Yalta conference in March 1945. The Soviets certainly did not need spies to tell them that the British and American stances at Yalta would be strongly affected by the Red Army's advance into Eastern Europe and by the American public's distaste—shared, with the exception of General George Patton, by its military leadership—for a new armed conflict with an ally that had done so much to defeat Nazi Germany. But if the geopolitical and military realities of 1945 had faded to some extent from public consciousness by the time Whittaker Chambers took the stand, so too had the political passions and social realities of the Great Depression, which accounted for much of the appeal of communist prescriptions for economic justice to American leftists (most of whom never joined the Party) in the thirties.

None of this, of course, had anything to do with the

question of whether Hiss was guilty, but it had a great deal to do with the demonization of those who had joined the Party for idealistic reasons and with the widespread public presumption in the late 1940s and 1950s that not only Hiss, but nearly everyone who had been a member of the Party, or even a fellow traveler, was guilty of moral, if not necessarily legal, treachery against the United States. As Cooke observed in 1950, "If we are now baited in every direction by the Russians, it does not satisfy Americans to say that this is the turn of history. It must mean that somebody entrusted with our welfare has betrayed or blundered."[8] In this climate of presumed treachery—established long before we knew what we know now about real Soviet espionage in the United States—it became easy to justify the violations of civil liberties that characterized the HUAC hearings, their imitators at the state level, and the entire McCarthyite crusade. And it became equally easy to dismiss the ruined lives of Americans guilty of nothing more than investing their youthful passion for social and economic justice in a Moscow-financed organization that—though it never made any real political headway among most Americans even during the worst period of the Depression—exploited their idealism for its own ends.

It is not my intention, in this slim volume, to reexamine or reevaluate the actual evidence in the Hiss case; anyone who wishes to do so will be better served by the works of scholars who have, mirabile dictu, devoted years of their lives to poring over documents so endless (and often so dull) that it would be impossible for anyone but a Cold War junkie to read them without going blind or mad. What remains important about the Hiss case today is its ability to strike chords located along ideological fault lines that, in spite of many cultural shifts, extend from the 1930s to the present. Where does dissent cross the line into disloyalty? When does an American government's determination to guard against treachery become a form of treachery to the Constitution, and to the very liberties the government is sworn to uphold? Should we trust what any government says, especially in the murky realm of espionage—a profession based by definition on trickery and filled with both accomplished and inept liars? And finally, what is the proper relationship of the United States to the international community? The contradictory historical scripts about the Hiss case reveal much more about conflicting visions of what America ought to be than about what American Communism actually was—or about who Alger Hiss was.

ONE

Passions as Prologue

We are about to look at the trials of a man who was
judged in one decade for what he was said to have done
in another.
—ALISTAIR COOKE, *A Generation on Trial*, 1950

It was not entirely true, even in 1950, that Alger Hiss was
being judged primarily on the basis of what he had done
in the 1930s. Unless a former Communist Party member
had thoroughly repudiated his past and turned against his
one-time friends and political associates, he was sus-
pected in the late forties and early fifties of still being a
secret Communist—or, at the very least, a communist
sympathizer known as a "fellow traveler."* In Hiss's case,

---

*The Russian word for "fellow traveler," *poputchik*, was coined in the early
Soviet era to describe intellectuals who were not Communist Party members
but who sympathized with and advanced the ideas of the Bolsheviks. The word
was not originally a pejorative, although many of the Russian intellectual poputchiki, after their usefulness to the Soviet regime had ended, disappeared during the purges of the thirties. In America after the Second World War, however, the term *fellow traveler* was always used as a pejorative.

the real suspicion underlying the indictment for perjury was that he had betrayed his country while serving as a State Department aide, by passing confidential information to the Soviets not only in the thirties but perhaps even during the Second World War (although Whittaker Chambers, who left the Party in 1938, never claimed to know anything about Hiss's subsequent activities). By the time Hiss was indicted and tried for perjury, he stood, in the opinion of a significant proportion of the public, for all of the American-born subverters-from-within who helped the Soviet Union to become the most prominent, indeed the only, counterweight to the power of the United States in the postwar world. To his liberal defenders, Hiss stood for all of the loyal Americans whose lives were being destroyed by charges that they had once been Communists or had even associated with Communists.

But it is impossible to understand the intensity of the passions surrounding the guilt or innocence of Hiss without making an imaginative leap backward to the thirties, when Americans were struggling with the Depression and trying to suppress awareness of the intermittent, still-distant signals of menace from Nazi Germany. During that decade, many American intellectuals were attracted to philosophical communism with a small c and to Soviet Communism as the only stalwart opponent of fascism in Europe. As the historian Richard Hofstadter notes, "the appeal of Communism during the 1930s was stronger among intellectuals than among any other stratum of the population; and . . . in a few spectacular instances, faith in Communism led to espionage."[1] Most intellectuals who were drawn to communism, regardless of whether they actually joined the Party, lacked firsthand knowledge about what life was really like in the Soviet Union under Joseph Stalin. These leftist intellectuals discounted reports of widespread famine in the countryside during the early thirties, and they later took the confessions and executions of old Bolsheviks during the purges at face value. But others on the left did recognize Stalinism for the evil that it was, especially after the purges and show trials of 1937 and 1938. Much of the enduring passion surrounding the Hiss case can be traced to the split in the thirties between pro-Soviet and anti-Soviet American leftists, and an astonishing number on both sides (indeed, nearly everyone capable of beginning a sentence with a capital letter and ending it with a period) have left exhaustive and sometimes exhausting memoirs repudiating or justifying their youthful selves. The sheer volume and intensity of these memoirs, many of which touch on the Hiss case in one way or another, have certainly had the effect of exaggerating the influence of communism on

American cultural life—and that is true whether one is talking about the actual importance of communism in the thirties, the retrospective importance attached to communism during the anti-Red crusades of the late forties and fifties, or the more distant, though not necessarily more dispassionate, historical evaluations offered today. Much of this exaggeration is the product of nothing more complicated than certain intellectuals' overestimation of their own importance. From reading the memoirs of the culture warriors of the Old Left—Irving Kristol, Irving Howe, Diana Trilling, Dwight Macdonald, and Edmund Wilson, to name only a few located at various points on the political spectrum—a Martian might understandably, and mistakenly, conclude that these people, largely unknown outside the left-wing intellectual pressure cooker in the northeast corridor running from Boston through New York to Washington, actually changed the course of world and American history. Writing in 1993, Trilling asserted:

> Today, with the defeat of Communism in Europe
> and its dissolution in the Soviet Union, it requires
> a considerable effort of historical memory to bring
> back to mind the extent to which Stalinism domi-
> nated American culture in the years before the

Second World War: in art, journalism, editing and
publishing, in the theater and the entertainment in-
dustries, in the legal profession, in the schools and
universities, among church and civic leaders, everywhere in our cultural life the Soviet Union exer-
cised a control which was all but absolute. The
submission to Stalinism by our opinion-forming
population was not always politically conscious. It
represented the fashionable trend in what was presumed to be enlightened thought.[2]

This statement is true only if "everywhere" extends from
the East River to the Hudson River and is bounded by
Greenwich Village on the south and Morningside Heights
on the north, allowing for outposts in Hollywood and
Harvard Yard. And it is true only if one accepts the
proposition that everyone attracted to Marxist ideology
in the thirties was also passionately attached to Stalin's
version of communism. It is equally crucial to recall that
for most of the thirties, the larger American public was as
indifferent to the left-wing political passions of intellectuals as it was to the right-wing passions of those who
already viewed communism as a serious threat. The House
Committee on Un-American Activities, then headed by
Representative Martin Dies, tried to stir up broad anti-

communist sentiment in the late thirties, but most Americans had other, more pressing concerns—such as how to make a living in a society where, in spite of the efforts of the New Deal, the economy was still troubled and the public's sense of economic security remained extremely fragile. (The Dies committee also investigated Nazi front organizations like the German-American Bund, but it paid much more attention to socialist and communist groups.) As the fateful year 1938 drew to a close, with England and France allowing Hitler to gobble up Czechoslovakia in a pursuit of the illusion of "peace in our time," fully 40 percent of Americans had never even heard of HUAC.[3] Although middle-class Americans undoubtedly had little esteem for communism (insofar as they thought about communism at all), the Soviet Union itself was not seen as a formidable adversary or as a major threat to world peace. In August 1937 the recently established Gallup Poll found that nearly three-quarters of Americans believed that there would be another world war—but only 11 percent thought that Russia would be responsible for starting the conflict.[4] Nearly one-third said that if a second world war broke out, Germany would be the instigator. Asked which side they would like to see win a war between Germany and Russia, 83 percent picked Russia.[5] That such views had been widely shared by Americans of all social classes in the thirties, and by nonintellectuals as well as left-wing intellectuals, was downplayed after the war by those who wished to portray all communists and fellow travelers as anti-American and as potential traitors.

It is true, as Hofstadter observed, that intellectuals were more active participants than most other Americans in left-wing causes, especially those involving foreign affairs. The Spanish Civil War, a matter of immense importance to intellectuals who correctly considered the conflict a testing ground for a future worldwide confrontation between communism and fascism, scarcely registered on the American public in 1937 and 1938. In 1937 Americans did not even rate the Spanish bloodletting among the ten most interesting news events of the year.[6] (The Sino-Japanese War, by contrast, was rated the second most interesting news event—after major floods in Ohio. Not surprisingly, the abdication of Britain's King Edward VIII and his marriage to the American divorcée Wallis Warfield Simpson—"the woman I love"—also ranked far ahead of the violence in Spain as a news event of compelling interest to the public.) Among the minority of Americans who *did* have strong opinions about the Spanish Civil War in 1937, 65 percent sympathized with the Spanish Republicans (also called Loyalists), backed by the Soviet Union. By 1938, when Soviet involvement on the Loyalist side and Nazi backing for the forces of Francisco Franco were much clearer, pro-Loyalist sentiment had risen to 75 percent among those who had an opinion. It is significant, however, that more than half of those polled still expressed no opinion on the issue.[7] Even the Roman Catholic Church, ideologically committed to fierce anticommunism because of the Soviet Union's official atheism and suppression of religious institutions, had only limited success in enlisting ordinary American Catholics in the anti-Red efforts of the thirties. The American Catholic hierarchy, which followed the lead of the Vatican in its support for Franco, invested considerable effort in persuading lay Catholics to follow the church's lead. Yet a 1938 Gallup Poll showed that in spite of the church's fervent propagandizing on behalf of Franco as the only alternative to a communist Spain, only 39 percent of American Catholics were firmly in the Franco camp. Another 30 percent supported the Loyalists, and the rest had no opinion.[8] (The chief difference between Catholics and non-Catholics was that more Catholics had an opinion, so the church hierarchy had been successful in raising consciousness of the issue on the part of the laity.) But most Americans, whatever their political views, were not about to follow the lead of impassioned young left-wingers by enlisting in the Abraham Lincoln Brigade to fight Franco's forces; they considered it more foolish than harmful for individuals to become involved in a European war. Nevertheless, it would have been hard to imagine in the thirties, given the relatively sanguine view of Soviet military intentions held by the majority of Americans before the 1939 Nazi-Soviet pact, that having participated in such causes as the Lincoln Brigade would be considered a badge of shame only a decade later. It was only after the Second World War, when a rich and triumphalist America emerged to confront the reality of Soviet domination over Eastern Europe, that anti-Red crusaders were able to tap into a rich popular vein of antiradical, antiforeign, antiatheist (for Soviet Communism was synonymous with atheism in the American mind), and, last but not least, anti-intellectual sentiment.

It is a significant measure of America's instant historical amnesia that Alistair Cooke, writing about the Hiss trials in 1950, already considered it imperative to remind his readers about the very different political and economic climate of the 1930s. Right from the start, the iconography of the Hiss case has been defined by cycles of memory and forgetting that seem extraordinarily compressed even by American standards of historical amnesia. "Ten years is a long time in the memory of any man," Cooke asserted in the opening chapter of *A Generation on*

Trial, titled "Remembrance of Things Past."[9] That depends on the age of the man. But ten years is not a long time in the memory of a nation, unless its fortunes have either improved or declined so dramatically that even the recent past grows dim. That is exactly what happened to America during the Second World War, which finally put an end to the Depression and aroused amply justified hopes, as a result of innovations like the GI Bill, of unprecedented prosperity and a previously unimaginable expansion of educational opportunity to what had been the blue-collar class. The rise of our recent ally the Soviet Union was the only serious source of insecurity, because Stalin's regime posed the only challenge to the postwar Pax Americana. Given the very different prewar popular mindset, it is unlikely, had Chambers leveled his public charges against Hiss in 1938 or 1939, that they would have attracted anything like the attention they did when they were presented before HUAC in 1948. Indeed, when Chambers privately told Assistant Secretary of State Adolf Berle in 1939 that Hiss, among other State Department officials, was a member of the Communist Party, Berle was not alarmed enough to launch a serious investigation. To the political right, Berle's failure to follow up on Chambers's charges is a significant and ominous indicator of the Roosevelt administration's leftist sympathies. But Roosevelt's State Department, like the rest of the country, was much more worried about Germany than about the Soviet Union—before and after the signing of the Nazi-Soviet pact.

Hiss himself was a political creature of the thirties, in that his left-wing political sympathies did not emerge before the Depression. Chambers, by contrast, embraced Bolshevism and joined the Party in 1925—the midpoint of a decade of prosperity in which even the tiny minority of Americans with left-wing political views could not imagine a future for communism in this country. By moving to the left not in the twenties but in the thirties, Hiss followed an entirely conventional course, dictated both by the nation's economic crisis and by personal ambition, for intellectuals of his generation.

In recent years, much of the conservative revisionist history of twentieth-century American liberalism has taken an essentially ahistorical point of view about the attraction of liberal intellectuals to communism in the thirties. From this perspective, liberals had to be naïve, stupid, or traitorous (often all three) to have failed to see through the terrorized Potemkin village that was Stalin's

Soviet Union. Such an analysis ignores that fact that intellectuals, like other Americans, were looking primarily at the state of their own nation in the early thirties, and what they saw was an undeniable crisis—not only of capitalism as an economic system but of American constitutionalism as a political system. Alger Hiss was twenty-eight years old on March 4, 1933, the day Franklin D. Roosevelt took his oath of office. The facts of the nationwide economic collapse, as unfamiliar to young Americans today as any battle described by Thucydides, were grim and terrifying. The official unemployment rate was around 25 percent, although that was probably an underestimate, because married women were generally left out of the calculus—even though many were looking desperately for any kind of work because their husbands had lost their jobs—and because so many people had lost their homes and were literally on the road, far from the reach of government statisticians. At any rate, the number of the officially unemployed, according to most analyses, was somewhere between thirteen million and seventeen million. On the Friday before Roosevelt's inauguration, the New York Stock Exchange suspended trading indefinitely. The United States Steel Corporation had laid off *all* of its full-time employees. More than five thousand banks had failed since the stock market crash of 1929, taking the life savings of millions of Americans with them. Each of these statistics represented broken lives. My maternal grandparents were among those who lost their houses as a result of the bank failures. My father, who turned nineteen just two weeks before FDR's inauguration, was forced to drop out of college because his family's savings were gone and his widowed mother had no means of support. In an excellent analysis of FDR's first hundred days, which proves that there is always something new to be said about the New Deal, *Newsweek*'s Jonathan Alter points out that the words *dictator* and *dictatorship* were frequently used with approval to describe what the new president ought to do to rescue the nation. The *New York Herald Tribune* covered the inauguration under the headline, "For Dictatorship if Necessary." Walter Lippmann, who spoke for the left-leaning political elite in the media, advised FDR in February, "The situation is critical, Franklin. You may have no alternative but to assume dictatorial powers."[10] That establishment figures, on both the left and the right, were talking about the necessity of abandoning constitutional restraints on executive power is a testament to the desperation of the times.

Five days before FDR's inauguration, Adolf Hitler— who has ascended to the chancellorship of Germany on January 30—moved to solidify Nazi power by successfully blaming German Communists for the burning of the Reichstag. The day after the inauguration, the Nazis and their supporters won a majority (albeit a small one) in a parliamentary election. These two forces—the continuing reality of the Depression at home and the rise of fascism abroad—would provide the backdrop for all American political discourse during the thirties.

In his 1988 memoir *Recollections of a Life*, Alger Hiss describes himself as an essentially apolitical, privileged young man before he encountered the social upheavals of the thirties. There is no reason not to believe him, nothing in his record to indicate that he was anything more than a bright young man from a Baltimore family of genteel background and pretensions but little money—and that he was determined to move up in society and in his chosen legal profession. "My views have altered less in the intervening half century than they did during the Depression years, especially 1931 and 32," Hiss writes. He describes his youthful moral code as "highly personal and quite formalistic" and says that "The Progress of a Prig" would be a "not too uncharitable" description of his personal and political development.

To be sure . . . I had a secondary and vague sense of
sympathy for those less fortunate than I. And I took
it for granted that "good works" (not specific) were
obligatory for self-respecting people. It was also, I
believed, a necessary though relatively minor function of any decent society to make some institu-
tionalized provision for the needy. Though this
latter went without saying, it also went without
much sense of responsibility on my part to see
whether that function was carried out. My sense
of social responsibility was complacently restricted.
And I think this was pretty much the content of the
social gospel of the churchgoing homeowners in the
modest Baltimore neighborhood where I grew up.
Decent social responsibility was to see that no one
starved, that the sick could have access to hos-
pital—at least on a charity basis—and that the
homeless had a shelter. This was hardly much improvement over the Poor Laws of the nineteenth
century, and was most inadequate for the cata-
strophic ills that came with the Great Depression.

At Harvard Law School, which he entered in 1926 after
receiving his bachelor's degree from Johns Hopkins University, Hiss encountered "the doctrine of disinterested,

dedicated public service for the first time."[11] That was certainly the doctrine embodied in the life and work of Hiss's mentor Felix Frankfurter. But although Hiss admired the impassioned commitment of Frankfurter to such causes as challenging the fairness of the trial accorded the Italian immigrant anarchists Nicola Sacco and Bartolomeo Vanzetti, executed in 1927, the young Hiss did not follow his mentor's path. When Hiss, after receiving his law degree, took the coveted job of secretary to Oliver Wendell Holmes, his primary aim was not to work for the betterment of mankind but to advance his career prospects (a generalization that applies to most law school graduates then and now). Hiss was an extremely good-looking young man, as indeed he would become a good-looking old man. His dark hair, slim frame, and patrician carriage—he would maintain the latter physical attributes into old age—bore the visual stamp of someone headed for success. Looking at a well-known 1930 photograph taken of Hiss with Holmes at the Supreme Court justice's summer house in Beverly Farms, Massachusetts, it would be easy to conclude that the twenty-six-year-old Hiss, in his three-piece suit, was the justice's son—and that the young man was destined for an eminence comparable to that of the older man. In Hiss's impeccable résumé from the 1920s, there is nothing to indicate that he was the sort of young man who would ever jeopardize his own future by engaging in out-of-the-mainstream political activities. The only unusual step Hiss took as a young man on the way up was his marriage to Priscilla Fansler Hobson, who had a young son by her first husband. Marrying a divorced woman in 1929 was not a move calculated to advance one's social or career prospects: Alger's mother reportedly sent him a telegram on the day of the wedding that warned, "Do Not Take This Fatal Step."[12] The young attorney was also violating Justice Holmes's well-known rule that his secretaries remain unmarried in order to devote their full attention to him. In a letter to Frankfurter about his wedding (which Hiss had concealed from Holmes until the last minute), Alger certainly displayed a talent for manipulation and prevarication. "I learned some ten hours before my marriage . . . that the justice had definitely stipulated that his secretaries be unmarried," Hiss told Frankfurter. "Of course, I appreciated that . . . the secretary's personal af fairs must never impinge a 'scintilla' on the justice's time or energy, and I—rather we—laid meticulous plans until the last moment. As part of these plans the justice was not informed until the last moment. . . . I in no wise sensed any fiat negative to marriage qua marriage—of incon-siderateness which might reasonably grow out of a sec-

retary's marrying he did gently complain, I suppose."[13]
What is striking about this letter is its slippery legalistic
tone; few twenty-five-year-olds, even those educated at
Harvard Law School, would be capable of coming up
with a tortuous sentence claiming that they "in no wise
sensed any fiat negative to marriage qua marriage." But
then, Hiss could hardly have said to Frankfurter, "I
wanted to get married, and I wanted to keep my job, and I
thought I could do it by lying to Justice Holmes as long as
possible." The historian G. Edward White interprets
Hiss's Artful Dodger behavior at the time of his marriage
as an indication that he was already "a person with a
strong belief in his ability to manipulate others, and perhaps with an underdeveloped appreciation of the risks of
being exposed. Even if one associates those characteristics
with many males in Hiss's age group . . . the choices Hiss
made seem unusual, and revealing."[14] This statement is a
typical example of the ex post facto analysis of Hiss's character in light of the subsequent accusations of spying. I
don't know how unusual, or unusually manipulative, it is
for any twenty-five-year-old to want to have his cake and
eat it too when it comes to fulfilling both his sexual de-
sires and his professional ambitions; it seems to me quite
a stretch from thinking that you can evade a crotchety old
boss's rule against marriage for staffers and thinking that

you can get away with being a Communist spy. In any case, Hiss's slightly unconventional marriage was the only thing he did in the 1920s that suggested any departure from the path of a clever young man on the make.

After his year with Holmes, Hiss took a job with a prestigious Boston law firm and two years later, in 1932, established himself with a similarly well-connected firm— Cotton, Franklin, Wright, and Gordon—in New York. It was during this period that Hiss, like so many well-educated Americans who had been chiefly engaged in feathering their own nests during the twenties, began to open his eyes to the misery around him. In 1930, while the Hisses were still living in Boston, Priscilla joined the Morningside Heights branch of the Socialist Party and began to engage in the seditious business of feeding the unemployed at soup kitchens on the Upper West Side. After moving to New York, Hiss began to do pro bono work for a group of lawyers called the International Juridical Association (IJA), established to assist attorneys representing workers and farmers hardest hit by the Depression. Hiss specialized in agricultural cases. By his own account, the work was an eye-opener.

The cases I read for the journal in 1932, which would not otherwise have come to my attention, made me realize how little access the victims of the Depression had to legal services and how little geared to their needs our legal system was. I learned that social justice also required political reform.

My work on that little journal likewise gave me a sense of identification with members of organized groups like labor unions and farm associations, who by joint efforts and with concrete social and political programs were actively trying to help themselves weather the Depression. Here was a sizable constituency urging reforms and prepared to support political action to gain them. Without realizing it, I was already indirectly in touch with the grass roots of the New Deal.[15]

The IJA, which would be described as a Communist-front organization during the hunt for Reds after the Second World War, was in reality one of the many associations (organization may be too organized a word to describe them) that sprang up in the early thirties, while the nation was sinking further into despair as the Hoover administration drew to a close. The IJA included liberals and leftists of many varieties, including Roosevelt Democrats who were neither socialists nor communists; socialists and communist sympathizers; and some who were already members of the Communist Party—or who would join the Party a few years later. Many lawyers who participated in the group, like other professionals who attempted to put their skills to use in an effort to address the nation's economic crisis, were employed at their day jobs by mainstream firms, where Roosevelt was viewed with emotions ranging from suspicion to outright hatred. Hiss was making six thousand dollars a year at his New York law firm—which put him on solidly upper-middle-class financial turf in 1933—and he did not have to take a pay cut when he went to work for the government. As his son, Tony, rightly observes, "There's always plenty of work for movie stars and lawyers in a depression."[16] There was nothing unusual, or especially deceptive, about a people-pleaser like Hiss moving with equal ease among moneyed clients who saw Roosevelt as "That Man" and among contemporaries who believed that American society must be radically transformed in order to ameliorate the worst effects of unconstrained capitalism. Allen Weinstein, whose book *Perjury* did so much to persuade many liberals of Hiss's guilt, considers it "doubtful" that Hiss became either a committed socialist or a Communist Party member during the early thirties; Weinstein suggests only that Hiss's political views shifted "leftward" (as Hiss himself indicates in his memoir).[17] In fact, the only striking thing about Hiss during this period was how much he resembled his contemporaries of comparable educational credentials and ambition. It would have been surprising had Hiss not been destined for a move to Washington as a junior member of the New Deal brain trust. As Hiss notes, his experiences in New York had made him fully receptive when he was offered a job in the spring of 1933 as assistant general counsel for the Agricultural Adjustment Administration (AAA), a key agency established during the New Deal's historic first hundred days. Frankfurter sent Hiss a telegram indicating that it was imperative for him to accept the Washington job "on basis national emergency." In discussing his decision to leave his law firm for government service, Hiss characteristically emphasizes both his similarities to and his superiority to many of his contemporaries. "My desire to follow the directive in Frankfurter's telegram was . . . prompt and wholehearted," he recalls.

> I was more ready for it than I realized. Here again, as with my participation in the International Juridical Association, I found that the views I had so recently reached and my inclination to act on them was shared by others of my age and with backgrounds quite like my own. But though I was not

the only young lawyer who went to Washington in that March of 1933, there were not all that many of us. We were entitled to think of ourselves—and we most certainly did—as a select few. I had this time taken a step or two in advance of the ranks of my generation, even of my close associates, though some of them came soon after.[18]

I was like others of my generation, but in the vanguard. This implicit boast permeates everything Hiss has ever written about himself, and it could certainly serve as an encomium for anyone who embraced many kinds of left-of-center politics during the thirties. Enthusiasm for the New Deal, however, was not a left-of-center position at all—though it might have looked that way to a man as conventional in his aspirations as Hiss seems to have been in the go-go 1920s before the stock market crash.

If Hiss was, in many ways, typical of the "best and the brightest" of his generation, his future accuser, Whittaker Chambers, was not. Chambers was anything but an "American icon," and the contrast between the scruffy witness with a history of overwrought political and religious enthusiasms and the polished, distinguished-looking lawyer and diplomat who had gone from success to success contributed substantially to the public fascination with and confusion about the case. While Hiss spent most of his twenties grooming himself and being groomed for professional success, Chambers, born in 1901, spent most of his twenties throwing away the conventional opportunities that came his way. Raised on Long Island in the seaside town of Lynbrook, Chambers was the product of an unconventional marriage in which his father, a graphic artist at the *New York World*, lived only intermittently with his mother. Chambers entered Columbia University in 1920 over the objections of his mother, Laha, who had wanted her son to attend an Ivy League institution with fewer Jews. Chambers, of course, was not Jewish, but his highly emotional demeanor, and the fact that he was married to a Jew, fitted the forties' stereotype of what leftists were thought to look like and sound like. Hiss, by contrast, looked like the Ur-WASP. While Hiss never missed a step in his progression from high school to college to law school, Chambers took a year off after high school graduation to escape his troubled family and earn his living as a railroad worker. He originally agreed to try Williams College, in Williamstown, Massachusetts, but took off for Columbia after only three days. The FBI's "Per-

sonal History" of Chambers's life reported that he had
skipped a freshman dinner to read the Bible and announced that "a great light" had dawned on him before
taking off for Columbia.[19] That sounds like the florid,
self-dramatizing Chambers of *Witness*, but I have a suspicion that the claustrophobia induced in an adventurous
young man by the isolation of Williamstown might have
had more to do with Chambers's flight to Morningside
Heights. Chambers's contemporaries at Columbia included an extraordinary number of intellectually gifted
young men, destined for distinction in academia and a variety of American cultural institutions. Among them
were Jacques Barzun, the future historian; Lionel Trilling, destined for veneration as a highbrow literary critic;
Meyer Schapiro, who would attain equal eminence as an
art critic; Mortimer J. Adler, who would help found the
"Great Books" series as a professor of philosophy at the
University of Chicago; and Clifton Fadiman, who would
become a Book-of-the-Month Club judge and host of the
popular radio quiz show *Information Please*. (Fadiman's career, somewhat to the dismay of the highbrows with
whom he had associated as a Columbia undergraduate,
placed him at the summit of middlebrow rather than high
culture in the late 1940s and 1950s.) Chambers not only
knew all of the brightest students among his Columbia

55

contemporaries; he was considered one of them. Most were (as his mother had feared) Jews, and they were the first Jews he had known on more than a casual basis. He was also the first gentile—at the time, he considered himself a Christian Scientist—treated as an equal by many of his Jewish contemporaries. All of these students fell under the spell of a young English instructor, Mark Van Doren, who combined intellectual adventurousness with WASP gentility. Chambers, who at that time despised communism, was a strong supporter of Calvin Coolidge—but that did not stop him from associating with friends on the political left. Chambers's contemporaries thought he might become an important novelist or poet. "We were convinced he [Chambers] would leap into fame," Barzun wrote Chambers's biographer Sam Tanenhaus in 1989.[20] But Chambers dropped out of Columbia during his junior year and, having briefly resumed his studies after a trip to Europe, finished with Columbia for good in December 1924. By that time he had discovered a new passion—communism—that replaced his former enthusiasm for silent Cal and the "business of America is business" Republicans. In February 1925 Chambers joined the Communist Party (then called the Workers Party of America). At that time, Bolshevism as a movement was unfashionable even among American intellectuals who had been enthusiastic about the victory of the Bolsheviks in Russia. Revolution was all very well for a country that had been ruled by tsars and the Russian Orthodox Church, but what did it all have to do with America? Not much. The idea that capitalism was doomed seemed ridiculous during the Roaring Twenties, and young academics working on their doctoral dissertations at Columbia, like law students pursuing their degrees at Harvard, were interested primarily in their own futures. When Chambers joined the Party, it had, at most, 16,000 members—and the vast majority were foreign born. Moreover, most Americans who did join the organized Bolshevik movement during the twenties made a swift exit from an organization whose chief activity was boring its members with Marxist-Leninist (or what were thought to be Marxist-Leninist) harangues. In 1928 the Party had no more than 10,000 official members, but it had registered 27,000 new members during the previous five years—the period when Chambers joined. Thus, two-thirds of those who joined the organized Communists in the mid-twenties left, in revolving-door fashion, in less than three years. Chambers, the True Believer, was an exception even among those who went so far as to join the Party—a member of a deeply committed minority within a minority of those who were trying on radical new political identities.[21] Chambers's old friends and literary acquaintances at Columbia—the ones who had predicted a brilliant literary future for him—were by turns amused, baffled, and condescending when they learned about his political commitment. Fadiman, who had introduced Chambers to *The Communist Manifesto* (which the Republican college freshman Chambers had described as a piece of "horrible rhetoric"), asked sarcastically, "Do you drill in a cellar with machine guns?" In *Witness*, Chambers would recall that "for the first time, I understood the contempt with which Communists pronounced the word 'intellectuals.' I thought: 'That miscellaneous mob in the English-speaking branch [of the Party] may not know the English language, but they know a good deal about history. They are not as intelligent as my college friends. But they do not think that ideas are ping-pong balls. They believe that ideas are important as a guide to coherent action." Communists, Chambers concluded, were "grown men and women," while his intellectual college friends were "children."[22]

While Chambers was writing for the dreary *Daily Worker*, the Party's informational organ, Hiss was reveling in being one of the select students invited to Frankfurter's Sunday teas in Cambridge, along with such luminaries as Judge Learned Hand; the intellectual journalist (and the journalist's intellectual) Walter Lippmann; and the economist Harold J. Laski. "After our host and his illustrious guests had expressed their views on whatever topic was under discussion," Hiss recalled, "Frankfurter would often turn to the students and say, 'And what do you think?' The query always left me momentarily speechless. One day he asked for my comments on Lord Acton's famous dictum that all power tends to corrupt, and absolute power corrupts absolutely. I had never heard the dictum before and could only come up with a lame observation, something to the effect that great ends call for great power."[23] This, by the way, is one of the many passages in Hiss's emotionally cool memoirs that make me doubt the veracity of much of his story. Hiss, in the recollection of all of his admirers, was a skilled conversationalist who was rarely unable to come up with observations that pleased others. Is it really possible that a Harvard law student had never heard Lord Acton's remark about power, which became a cliché almost as soon as it was written in 1887? Would the brilliant Frankfurter have chosen such a poorly educated and slow-witted protégé? And why does it suit Hiss to describe himself as something of a naïf in his memoir? Unlike Chambers's *Witness*, which has a passionate, somewhat demented authenticity in its recall of the author's religious conversion to communism, Hiss's slim memoir sounds like the labored effort of an old man who has no gut-level memory of what he really felt as a young man. How did it possibly happen that the incautious and extreme Chambers and the classic climber Hiss ever managed to meet, much less share the same ideas and become friends (according to Chambers) or even acquaintances (according to Hiss)?

If Weinstein is right, and Hiss was nothing more than a cautious fellow traveler in the early 1930s, Hiss and Chambers would certainly never have crossed paths in New York. By 1932, when he went underground as a spy for the Soviets, Chambers was a well-known Communist writer—the editor of the *New Masses* and a contributor to many other far-left publications. Like many Communists and fellow travelers, Chambers also maintained his connection to the expanding world of middlebrow culture. He never lost track of his old classmates from Columbia, in spite of his disdain for their unwillingness to take political action by joining the Party. His old friend Fadiman, an editor at the hot new publishing house of Simon and Schuster, hired Chambers, who was fluent in German, to translate *Bambi*, by the Austrian novelist Felix Salten. In the spring of 1932, Chambers became editor of *New Masses* for the munificent sum of fifteen dollars a week (13 percent of Hiss's salary). To his job at the Communist magazine, which published such writers as Katherine Anne Porter, John Dos Passos, and Edmund Wilson, Chambers brought a determination not to slight either political content or literary quality. His mission was to seduce the poputchiki—the very sorts of intellectuals who had been his friends at Columbia—in the hope that their literary talents would draw in new readers who might have rejected a purely political publication. In Chambers's view,

> These were the years that floated Alger Hiss into the party and made possible the big undergrounds, the infiltration of the Government, science, education and all branches of communications, but especially radio, motion pictures, book, magazine and newspaper publishing. An entirely new type of Communist made his appearance, not singly but in clusters, whose members already knew one another, influenced one another and shared the same Communist or leftist views. A surprising number came of excellent native American families. Nearly all were college trained from the top per cent of their classes. Those who lacked the hardihood or clarity to follow the logic of their position and become Communists clumped around the edges of the party, self-consciously hesitant, apologetic, easing

their social consciences by doing whatever the party asked them to do so long as they did not have to know exactly what it was.[24]

It is impossible to describe these years from Alger Hiss's perspective, not only because he denied having had a Communist past until the end of his life but because everything he ever published is almost entirely devoid of passion—either about shattering private events or about the personal impact of great public events. From Hiss's writings, a reader learns as little about his feelings about the suicide of his father (when Alger was only five) as about his emotional response to the heady conviction of so many of his contemporaries in the thirties that "a better world's in birth." Was Hiss's heart ever stirred by the words of the Communist anthem, the "Internationale," or were his political convictions purely a matter of intellect? One of the most psychologically revealing passages in Hiss's memoir is his account of the first time he learned that his father had killed himself, and it is truly astonishing that in the reevaluations of the case over the past twenty years (by sympathetic as well as hostile observers), so little has been made of Hiss's peculiar description of the impact of his father's suicide on the family. Hiss talks about his feelings almost entirely in terms of how things looked to others—and the need to keep the family secret within the family.

I did not know that my father had taken his own life until I was about ten years old and I overheard the remark of a neighbor sitting on her front steps talking with another neighbor. As my younger brother and I passed by, we hear her say, "Those are the children of a suicide."

Donald and I had been shielded from the shameful act; and there was not even a hint of a family secret. . . . The tragedy that had overwhelmed the household had been relegated to the sphere of nonexistence. Consequently, I was angered by the callous remark that I believed to be false and insulting. It remains one of my most painful and indelible memories.

On the whole, however, my childhood memories are of a lively and cheerful household, full of the bustle of constant comings and goings. . . .

I recognized that my mother and the other adults in my life had known of the suicide, but somehow I did not feel resentment at having been kept in the dark. Once I had learned the adult secret, I joined in the family policy of silence.[25]

The only thing Hiss resented, if one is to take this passage at face value, was the fact that outsiders knew the truth about his father.

Hiss's recollections of his young manhood, both in New York and in Washington, are characterized by a comparable lack of emotional affect. This absence is genuinely odd, because the 1930s, like the 1960s, left an indelible emotional as well as intellectual mark on all who were young and politically aware. To read memoirs by other survivors of internecine left-wing political wars of the thirties, from Irving Kristol (who become the patriarch of the Jewish neoconservatism that emerged from the anti-Stalinist Old Left) to Irving Howe (equally anti-Stalinist, but a man who never gave up his allegiance to democratic socialism), is to realize anew how exciting it must have been to be young at a time when many people believed that political ideas could transform an unjust world. Hiss's account of his work for the IJA journal is about as stirring as an office inventory of supplies in storage closets. Hiss does not even mention any of the people in the IJA by name; there is no sense of how common it was for liberals, socialists, and communist sympathizers to cooperate on a wide variety of social, political, and artistic enterprises. Did they enjoy one another's company? Did they argue? Did they ever drop by a speakeasy after work and enjoy an illegal drink while they talked about the day's business? Hiss's failure to address these quotidian questions is, I suppose, unsurprising for someone whose first life became the center of a historical debate.

One must turn to other sources—generally people who did not deny their old communist sympathies even though they had long since repudiated them—for a sense of the heady idealism, whether misplaced or not, of the times. Chambers's description of fellow travelers who "clumped around the edges of the party" is supported by Diana Trilling in an unintentionally comical account in her 1993 memoir, *The Beginning of the Journey.* Diana, whose only real career in the early thirties was being the wife of Lionel Trilling, joined the National Committee for the Defense of Political Prisoners (NCDPP) in 1932. The committee, a fellow-traveling organization that included many Communist Party members, became well known in 1933 for its involvement in the infamous case of the Scottsboro Boys, nine black teenagers charged in Alabama with the rape of two white prostitutes.* Trilling, who says she never heard the name Alger Hiss until

*The U.S. Supreme Court reversed the convictions twice on procedural grounds. At a second trial, one of the white women recanted her testimony. Charges were eventually dropped against five of the nine defendants, and the others were declared eligible for parole. In 1976 the last surviving Scottsboro

Chambers launched his spectacular charges in 1948, did know Chambers, who had never lost touch with his college classmate Lionel. She also knew that Chambers was a Communist Party member and some sort of spy. In 1933 Chambers visited Trilling at home and asked her to receive mail for him—to be, in the language of espionage tradecraft, his "drop." Trilling, who, whatever her political convictions, was a timid soul when it came to sticking out her own neck, was nevertheless flattered by the invitation. "With good reason, I regarded myself as preternaturally fearful, yet here was this man of the world, this man of two worlds, who believed me to be courageous enough to be a semi-spy. I felt greatly complimented." Looking for a way to say no to Chambers without offending him, Trilling was rescued by a fortuitous phone call informing her that her father's best friend had committed suicide by sticking his head in a gas oven. (She reports the fortuitousness of this call without a trace of irony: the suicide of a friend was one way to say no to a Communist

---

defendant, Clarence Norris, was pardoned by, of all people, Governor George Wallace. Norris had broken parole and fled the state in 1946. The Communist Party played an important role in the defense of the Scottsboro Boys. Although Diana Trilling is undoubtedly right to assert that the Party was interested chiefly in dramatizing the plight of blacks under capitalism, a historian today might reasonably ask, "So what?" It is something of an understatement to say that among "centrist" whites in the thirties, there was little interest in the legal plight of blacks in the South. The Party knew a vacuum when it saw one.

spy, or put off the refusal, without appearing to be rude.) Then Chambers, whose younger brother had committed suicide, comforted Trilling and apparently went on his way without any more discussion of her potential services as a conspirator.[26] This account not only demonstrates what a muddleheaded young woman Diana Trilling was (though not silly enough to actually agree to become an accomplice to a spy) but also captures the matter-of-fact nature of relations between fellow travelers and the Communist Party in the thirties—at least in New York. The account underscores the truth of Alistair Cooke's observation about the vast change in standards of political judgment between the decade that preceded the Second World War and the decade that followed it.

The Trillings' leftist trajectory was somewhat out of joint with many of their intellectual contemporaries, because they were closest to the Party (though they never actually joined) in the early thirties. For most intellectuals the pull of communism became much stronger during the period from the mid-thirties, with the rise of Nazism, until the signing of the Nazi-Soviet nonaggression pact in August 1939. These were the years of the Popular Front, when the

Soviets ostensibly dropped their objection to noncommunist leftist movements in order to make common cause against fascism. Membership in the American Communist Party rose steadily, and the Party drew in not only intellectuals but communist sympathizers in certain unions. At a time when many Americans underestimated the threat of Nazism and most were committed isolationists, the Popular Front had enormous appeal to intellectuals who saw Hitler (but not Stalin) for the evil creature that he was. The vast majority never joined the Party, and participation in organizations or literary endeavors sympathetic to Soviet-backed causes—the most urgent and appealing being opposition to Nazism—was the most common form of fellow traveling for intellectuals. Among the general public, by contrast, communism was even less popular in the mid-thirties than it had been at the beginning of the New Deal. With the nation still in dark economic straits in 1936, Americans overwhelmingly reelected Franklin D. Roosevelt; the tiny Communist Party vote dropped from 0.3 percent to 0.2 percent of the electorate, while the American Socialist Party, always much stronger at the ballot box than the Communists, dropped from 2.2 percent to 0.4 percent. It would seem obvious that most citizens, even if they were still enduring personal economic hardship, had taken heart and hope from the New Deal.

Intellectuals, however, were more concerned than other Americans about the rise of fascism in Europe (in part because Jews were disproportionately represented among left-wing intellectuals). This was also the period when a sharp split began to emerge between Communists and anti-Communist liberals, the latter group including such disparate men as the progressive educator John Dewey and the philosopher Sidney Hook, who had been a Marxist and a supporter of the Communist candidate for president in 1932. In spite of their history of communist sympathies, intellectuals like Dewey and Hook were not deceived when Stalin branded one old Bolshevik after another as a traitor and disposed of both real and imaginary opponents in the purge trials of 1937 and 1938. There were also younger leftists who never flirted with Stalin's version of communism; the best descriptions of what it was like to be a fledgling soldier in the irregular army of the anti-Stalinist left are to be found in Irving Howe's and Irving Kristol's memoirs of their sentimental political educations at the City College of New York from 1936 to 1940.[27] Howe and Kristol were on the same side back then, although Kristol would become the hardest of hardline neoconservatives in the 1970s, while Howe would, to a considerable extent, remain true to the democratic socialist ideals of his youth instead of rejecting them as guileless unrealism. The anti-Stalinists held forth in alcove 1 of the City College lunchroom, and the Stalinists made their pronouncements from alcove 2, whose denizens included Julius Rosenberg, destined to become one of only two Americans (the other was his wife, Ethel) executed for spying. Howe's description, perhaps befitting a democratic socialist, makes alcove 1 sound like a fairly jolly forum.

> You could walk into the thick brown darkness of
> Alcove 1 at almost any time of day or evening and
> find a convenient argument about the Popular
> Front in France, the New Deal in America, the civil
> war in Spain, the Five-Year Plan in Russia, the theory of permanent revolution, and "what Marx really
> meant." . . . One friend, Izzy Kugler, had a large
> body of knowledge and near knowledge. In a clash
> with a Stalinist boy whom we had lured across the
> border into Alcove 1, Izzy bombarded him with
> figures about British imperialism, and when the
> poor fellow expressed disbelief, Izzy sternly directed him to the library where he could "look it
> up." A fact was a fact. But had Izzy really been
> hammering him with facts? I asked about those
> statistics and he answered with a charming smile

that, well, he had exaggerated a little (which is to
say, a lot), since you had to do *something* to get those
Stalinist sluggards to read a book![28]

But for many intellectuals—even if they were not actually
Party members—it took the 1939 Nazi-Soviet pact, which
allowed Hitler to gobble up Poland and thereby ushered
in World War II, to reveal Stalin's absolute cynicism. Even
so, after Hitler attacked Russia, and the United States entered the war on the side of the Soviets and Great Britain,
Soviet-led communism regained the loyalty of many. Although the Party had lost nearly half of its American
members (especially Jews) after the Nazi-Soviet pact, it
doubled in size from 1941 to 1944, reaching a high point
of about eighty thousand members.[29]

In the years between Hitler's takeover of total power in
Germany and the Nazi-Soviet pact, it is impossible to
overestimate the importance of the rise of Nazism in
turning fellow travelers into Party members. The Marxist
literary critic Granville Hicks, who replaced Whittaker
Chambers as editor of *New Masses* when Chambers went
underground as a spy, did not join the Party until 1935,
and the ascendancy of Hitler was his main reason for becoming a committed, albeit sometimes uneasy, member.
"That capitalism could evolve into fascism was the final

demonstration that it must be abolished," Hicks wrote in 1941 (by which time he had left the Party). "And we thought it no accident that Hitler had struck first against the Communists, for they had been his most militant enemies. Indeed, we fellow travelers believed the Communists when they claimed to be the only effective fighters against the fascist threat."[30]

Fellow travelers like Hicks excused the American Communist Party when it attempted to denigrate the sincerity and effectiveness of Socialist and liberal opposition to fascism. In February 1934 the American Socialist Party (which had a much larger membership than the Communist Party) held a rally in Madison Square Garden to protest Austrian Chancellor Engelbert Dollfuss's ruthless suppression of a Socialist uprising. (Dollfuss himself would be assassinated by Austrian Nazis in 1935.) American Communists, indignant at very suggestion that Socialists might be considered leading opponents of fascism, marched en masse to the Garden, booed Mayor Fiorello H. La Guardia, who was sitting on the platform, and turned the peaceful protest into a riot. (The presence of the mayor of New York at a Socialist rally, by the way, is yet another indication of the very different tenor of politics in the thirties than in the postwar era.) American Socialists had a long history of being attacked from both the left and the right. In November 1918, shortly after the signing of the armistice that ended the First World War, another Socialist rally in Madison Square Garden was broken up by angry veterans who confused the Socialists with Communists. The veterans had to be subdued by mounted police, and the fact that Socialists detested Bolsheviks meant nothing to the rioters. The tendency of nonintellectual Americans to lump socialism and communism together was well established by the end of the First World War, and this conflation infuriated left-wing intellectuals of every stripe. How could those stupid bourgeois citizens not know the difference between a Stalinist and a Trotskyist? For an orthodox Communist, the sheer stupidity of the American public was responsible for the heretical notion that socialism might also be a revolutionary political doctrine. Fellow travelers like Hicks, who later reported that he had been appalled in 1934 at the violent Communist tactics directed against Socialists, nevertheless made no public protest—a silence typical of intellectuals who sympathized with Bolshevism in the thirties.

"Public criticism, then," Hicks recalled, "could only aid those whose faults seemed to me much worse than the party's, and I had to content myself with private protest." Communist sympathizers like Hicks were convinced that their private protests had been heeded when, in 1935, the Seventh Congress of the Communist International proclaimed the Popular Front and ostensibly dropped opposition to collaboration between Communists and non-Communist leftists in the fight against fascism. The effect of the Popular Front was to make the American Communist Party a much more comfortable place for leftists of all kinds. As Hicks notes, the survivors "of all factional fights, who had read nothing but the Marxist classics and the *Daily Worker,* dutifully began to read American history and literature, and were surprised to find they were learning something." Although some of the older Party members were upset, Hicks reports that "most of them were glad to relax and be human, and it was a surprise to themselves as to others to discover how human they could be." The famous organizer Mother Bloor was reported to have said at a birthday party, "Thank God I have lived to see a little sentiment in the Communist party!"[31]

Sentimentality would have been a more apt term. It seems highly probable that the emotional and the political relaxation permitted by the Communist International's declaration of the Popular Front would have drawn not only fellow-traveling New York intellectuals but a New Dealer like Hiss much closer to the Party. Barely a month after the International endorsed the Popular Front policy, Hiss left his job as counsel to a Senate subcommittee, headed by Republican Senator Gerald P. Nye of North Dakota, investigating the immense profits made by arms manufacturers—"merchants of death"—during the First World War. The majority of the Nye committee, like the majority of Americans, was determined that the United States remain neutral in future European conflicts. Hiss says he resigned because the endorsement of neutrality by the committee "seemed to encourage a passive attitude on our part toward Hitlerism."[32] The Popular Front not only permitted but encouraged cooperation between American Communists, left-wing elements in American labor, and liberal New Dealers. Such policies allowed Communists to reach out to government officials like Hiss and to middle-class intellectuals, and it allowed liberals of many varieties to see Communists as their allies in the effort to wake up the American people to the menace of fascism. After leaving the Nye committee, Hiss moved first to the Justice Department and then, in 1936, to the State Department. It was during this period that men like Hicks actually joined the Party and accepted a mindset that would subordinate all doubts, including those aroused by the purge trials, to their conviction that the fascist threat was more important than any other political issue. "In fact, I was smug and superior toward those who had nothing better to do than to try to exonerate Trotsky while I was raising money for Spain and helping to build the labor movement," Hicks writes. "Thus I took the hurdle of the trials as I had taken that of the Madison Square Garden riot, never suspecting that there would be a higher hurdle that would trip me up."[33] The higher hurdle, of course, was the Nazi-Soviet pact.

Communism has so often been described as a religion, especially by intellectuals who lost their Bolshevik faith, that it is tempting to search for a definition that is less of a cliché. Yet there is no doubt that for many American intellectuals (Chambers among them), communism served the same emotional needs that other religions do. And by the late thirties, retaining belief in the moral superiority and objective effectiveness of communism required something else characteristic of all traditional faiths: imperviousness to evidence. Yet there was another way in which communism resembled religion: the movement had its passionate fundamentalists and its cooler, more skeptical participants. Men like Chambers were the fundamentalist evangelicals of American Communism, and men like Hicks were the Unitarians and Reform Jews. Assuming that Hiss was a committed communist, he surely belonged to the cooler, more analytical precincts of the faith. And in these cooler precincts, particularly during the years of the Popular Front, many believers saw no inevitable contradiction between communism and support for the New Deal—just as they (along with most non-communists) would see no contradiction between American patriotism and support for the Soviets as an ally during the war. Obviously, no one will ever know what Hiss was thinking when he handed over government documents to Chambers, a.k.a George Crosley, a.k.a. the underground agent "Carl" in the 1930s. But it is almost as difficult to discern from his writings what he really thought about subjects that did not require him to admit to having been a Communist. Consider his baffling observations about Stalin at Yalta:

> As I look back on the Yalta Conference after more than forty years, what stand out strikingly are the surprising geniality as host and the conciliatory attitude as negotiator of Joseph Stalin, a man we know to have been a vicious dictator. . . .
>
> Our preoccupation with Stalin was understandable. From reliable intelligence sources we knew, as the public generally did not, of many of Stalin's monstrous crimes against his people. He was like a tyrant out of antiquity. But we also knew of his adroit skill

as a negotiator and his evident success as a war
leader. . . .

During breaks in the talks, Stalin carried himself
without any seeming pride of place. He stood in the
lavatory line with his aides and the rest of us lesser
fry while Churchill was taken to [Secretary of
State] Stettinius's suite and Roosevelt went to his
own. His aides spoke to him casually. His erect carriage and stolidity nonetheless gave him a touch of
aloofness and reserve.[34]

Hiss was too much of a gentleman, one assumes, to reveal
how Stalin measured up physically in a line of urinals occupied mainly by "lesser fry." There is something quin-
tessentially American about the emphasis on appear-
ances, and that is true whether one reads the passage as an
honest attempt to refute the long-held right-wing contention that Roosevelt gave away the store to the Russians
at Yalta or as a piece of propaganda designed to leave the
impression that the Soviet Union, not the United States,
made most of the concessions. Who knows? Perhaps if
Hiss had never really heard Lord Acton's dictum about
power before hearing it at the Frankfurter salon, he was
also innocent of the knowledge that a man "may smile,
and smile, and be a villain." (Hiss is quite right, however,

in his assertion that Roosevelt's primary objective at Yalta was to gain a firm commitment for Soviet entry into the war against Japan. Right-wing critics of the Yalta agreement have focused on what the United States did not get—any concessions from Stalin that might have led to the formation of an independent, democratic Poland. None of these analysts has ever explained exactly what the United States could have done, short of attacking the Soviet troops that already occupied much of Poland, to make Stalin cede control of land that had served as an attack corridor into the Soviet Union for the Nazi armies.)

Hiss's Washington journey from the AAA, one of the most innovative agencies established at the outset of the New Deal, to the State Department, a bastion of traditionalism in spite of its New Deal component, could have been nothing more than the rising trajectory of a committed careerist. But it was also a trajectory well suited to the aims of Soviet espionage agents in the United States, who hoped to penetrate the more traditional government agencies, like the State, War, and Treasury Departments, with young New Dealers sympathetic to the Soviet Union (whether or not they were actually members of the Party). Chambers, among others, would testify that the eventual penetration of the government was the ultimate aim of a group initially overseen in Washington by Hal

Ware, a Communist and the son of Mother Bloor, who had rejoiced in the "sentiment" that the Popular Front had engendered in the Party. Hiss, Chambers would testify, was a member of the Ware group. When members did succeed in moving up the government ladder, they were supposed to separate from the Ware organization, which was well known for its Marxist participants. Chambers was dispatched from New York by underground Party superiors to supervise and coordinate the transmission of information and to ride herd on underground Communists—Hiss among them—with government jobs. A consistent theme of many of Hiss's defenders from the sixties on would be that Chambers had never been a Soviet spy—that his account of his secret life as an agent was as delusional as his claim of having been a close friend of Alger and Priscilla Hiss.

In any event, both communism and fellow-traveling in Washington were very different from the open leftist intellectual brew in New York. Casual and social association between avowed Communists and noncommunist leftists was rare in the nation's capital. If there had been an equivalent of the Trilling household in Washington, Whittaker Chambers would most certainly not have turned up on the doorstep and asked to use the place as a "drop." All of the early initiatives of the New Deal were being de-

nounced by conservatives as forms of, or steps on the road
to, socialism and communism. And conservatives did not
respect, recognize, or care about the distinctions between
the communist and noncommunist left that were of such
immense importance to intellectuals. In New York, one
might be both a communist and a journalist, or a communist and a social worker, or a communist and a composer
of Broadway songs, but one could not be an open communist and a government official in the District of Columbia. Furthermore, Washington—in spite of the expansion
of the federal government engendered by the New
Deal—was basically a small southern town in the 1930s.
Whether you were flirting with a mistress or the Communist Party, the chances of running into someone you
knew anywhere in Washington were infinitely greater
than the chances of running into someone you knew in
New York. Chambers claims to have met Hiss for the first
time in 1934 at a cafeteria on Pennsylvania Avenue, at a
lunch arranged by Josef Peters, who had been trained in
Moscow to supervise underground American Communist Party operations. (Peters, generally referred to as "J.
Peters" in histories of American Communism, was a
Hungarian who joined the Party in his native land in
1918.) Chambers recalled that the cafeteria "was located
(rather fittingly) a few doors from the Washington

Post."* This public venue, also located near the Department of Agriculture, strikes me as an odd choice for any meeting involving Hiss, because Peters was a distinctive, foreign-looking figure, complete with bushy eyebrows and a prominent mustache. Chambers was a seedy-looking, slightly pudgy, ill-dressed man with rotting teeth in need of major dental work. Neither Peters nor Chambers looked like the sort of people whom Hiss would have been expected to choose as lunch companions (although Chambers's teeth could easily have been those of the impoverished sharecroppers whom Hiss tried to help as a lawyer for the AAA). Had Hiss run into his boss, Jerome Frank, or any of his live-wire colleagues from the AAA— who included Adlai Stevenson; Telford Taylor, who would gain fame as a prosecutor at the Nuremberg war crimes trials; Abe Fortas; and Thurman Arnold—he would have had trouble explaining what he was doing with characters who looked more like Groucho Marx (Peters) or one of the Three Stooges (Chambers) than like respectable professionals doing business with the government. By that time, Hiss had already taken on an additional assignment

*The reference to the *Post* presumably indicates Chambers's belief that the newspaper, like all liberal media, had pinko sympathies. The owner at the time, Eugene Meyer (grandfather of the present chairman of the company, Donald L. Graham), had made a fortune on Wall Street and had been chairman of the Federal Reserve during the last two years of Herbert Hoover's administration before buying the newspaper.

as counsel to the Nye committee on munitions profits, and—assuming he was a Communist—he could hardly have been unconcerned about the possibility of running into someone he knew from Capitol Hill. (Important people rarely frequent cafeterias—or their debased successors, fast-food restaurants—today, but that was not true in Washington from the thirties through the early sixties. The Scholl's chain of cafeterias—and I'd be willing to bet money that the place Chambers recalled was a Scholl's—was an institution that, like the Automat in New York, was frequented by members of all social classes.)

To be a committed Communist Party member in Washington in the thirties would inevitably have meant loneliness, duplicity, and social isolation. We can never know what Hiss felt about this double life, because he asserted that the duality was a pure fiction invented by Chambers, "a possessed man and a psychopath."[35] And Chambers was also a closeted, married homosexual fighting his attraction to men while, by his own admission, engaging in one-night stands with strangers in hotels in Washington, Annapolis, Maryland, and New York City. Chambers claimed that he managed to suppress his homosexual impulses, with the help of God, at the same time that he left the Communist Party in 1938. In Hiss's view, implied rather than stated forthrightly, he may have been as much the victim of a frustrated crush as of Chambers's political delusions. "I now believe that my rebuff to him wounded him in a way I did not realize at the time," Hiss says delicately.[36] That may well be. I look at the pictures of Hiss and Chambers from the 1930s, and I think that the handsome, elegant, professionally successful, and self-confident Hiss could not have been anything but another source of torment—an unattainable object of desire—for the scruffy-looking, financially struggling, emotionally tortured Chambers. When Hiss finally admitted to knowing Chambers (though only as the freelance journalist George Crosley, a seeker of information about the investigations of the Nye committee), he said that Crosley's financial struggles had aroused his sympathy. Thus he explained his small loans to Chambers, his subletting an apartment to Chambers and his wife, and his gift of an old Ford, about to be discarded because Hiss was buying a new car. When Hiss finally broke off his relationship with Chambers, he ascribed the breach to his realization that Chambers had no intention of ever paying back any of the money he had borrowed. Chambers, of course, said that *he* was the one who broke with Hiss by leaving the Party. One inescapable conclusion can be drawn from these conflicting stories: Hiss was far above Chambers in social and professional standing. In fact, Hiss is an iconic figure for another, frequently overlooked reason: he was one of a minority of Americans who prospered during the Depression and ended the 1930s in much better economic positions than they had occupied in the 1920s. It truly is an ill wind that blows nobody good, and Americans in such divergent occupations as bartending and law profited in what were the worst of times for many of their countrymen. Lawyers belonged to a professional class whose economic standing improved slowly but continuously throughout the Depression; the expansion of the public sector during the New Deal provided more legal work for both government and private attorneys.

What could possibly have explained the willingness of an up-and-coming New Deal lawyer to lend money to, and find housing for, a down-and-out figure like Chambers? In his memoir, Hiss says only that Crosley-Chambers was "good company for a while" and "well read . . . stereotypically the proletarian writer so much celebrated in those days . . . a latter-day Jack London."[37] Hiss basically attributes his willingness to help Chambers to the kindness of his own heart. This explanation makes perfect sense to Hiss's younger generation of defenders. Jeff Kisseloff, managing editor of the pro-Hiss Web site sponsored by the Nation Institute, first met Hiss in the 1970s and writes, "If you walked the streets with Alger, you soon learned, as Whittaker Chambers did in the 1930s, that he was the easiest mark in the world. When a beggar would approach with a hand out, Alger would not just pull a fistful of change from his pocket, he'd invariably ask, 'Is that enough?' Would he have tossed in his old Ford when he sublet his apartment to Chambers in 1935? You bet."[38] Kisseloff's impressions of Hiss as an "easy mark" run somewhat counter to the image of Hiss as a man who, according to his trial testimony, ended his relationship with Chambers when he realized that the loans were never going to be repaid. But perhaps Hiss found it easier to be generous to anonymous beggars than to people he actually knew. Chambers, of course, says Hiss helped him out because they were both Communists—and that communism was at the heart of their friendship.

Hiss, although he had a first-rate education and a first-rate legal mind, was not—at least not in the thirties—an intellectual with the wide-ranging interests of Chambers's old friends at Columbia. "Compared to the minds I had grown up with at Columbia," Chambers recalled, "free ranging, witty and deeply informed (one only has to think of Clifton Fadiman or Meyer Schapiro), Alger was a little on the stuffy side. Ideas for their own sake did not interest him at all. His mind had come to rest in the doctrines of Marx and Lenin, and even then applied itself wholly to current politics and seldom, that I can remember, to history or theory."

I particularly remember Alger's opinion of Shakespeare. In 1936 or 1937, Maurice Evans played *Richard II* in Baltimore. It was the first time that my wife or I had ever seen Shakespeare acted. We were deeply impressed, not only by the new life the play took on for us on the stage, and the new texture given the verse by Evans's elocutionary style, but by the aliveness of the politics of the play. During the opening scenes, my wife whispered to me with awe: "It's just like the Comintern!"

A day or so later, I was trying to convey some of that to Alger. "I'm sorry," he said at last, somewhat less graciously than usual, "I just don't like Shakespeare —platitudes in blank verse." He quoted some Polonius, and I realized, for the first time with great interest, that he disliked Shakespeare because the platitudes were all that impinged on his mind.[39]

It will doubtless be objected that it is unfair to Hiss to allow Chambers to define him. Indeed, Hiss's son, Tony, contemptuously quotes the same passages from Chambers's book, which he calls a "nonfiction novel." To counter Chambers's unflattering intellectual portrait of his father,

Tony Hiss quotes many letters his father wrote his mother while serving his prison sentence for perjury. "Does thee remember a search we made in 1945 for poems of stature on peace?" Hiss asked his wife, using the Quaker form of address.

> And how we found that our inability to recall any was due to their virtual non-existence. Man has never been sufficiently at peace within himself to have any vigorous + concrete concept of peace with his fellows. Similarly, there is a dearth of words to express the affirmative outreach + aspiration of spirit which is the natural accompaniment + source of human growth + maturation. The obstacles to realization of man's potentialities have been so overwhelming that the most articulate + whole men of history have never, until very recent times, grasped those visions of potentialities except in mystical raptures which were largely uncommunicable. In stating the problem I have almost exhausted the common vocabulary of fully realized human growth."[40]

If Hiss's philosophy in the thirties was similar to that expressed in this letter from prison in 1952, it does not contradict the portrait drawn by Chambers or, indeed, the picture that emerges in Hiss's own public writings. A

man who really believes there is a "dearth of words to ex-
press the affirmative outreach + aspiration of spirit which
is the natural accompaniment + source of human growth
+ maturation" can hardly have been well acquainted with
Shakespeare. Or, for that matter, with lesser but widely
read English-language poets. How did Hiss get through
elementary and high school without being forced by some
teacher to memorize Tennyson's "Locksley Hall," imag-
ining a future of international cooperation—"Till the war
drum throbbed no longer and the battle flags were furled /
In the Parliament of man, the Federation of the world"?

But this passage from the prison letter does shed much
more light than Hiss's public writings on his philosophical cast of mind—the idealistic bent that led so many
well-intentioned men and women to link communism
with world peace in the thirties. For the most part, we
hear nothing but 20-20 hindsight sneers today for the
thirties' leftists who did not see through the Soviet
Union, who discounted reports of famine and purges as
anticommunist propaganda, who justified the Nazi-Soviet pact (having excoriated Britain and France for failing
to stand up to Hitler), and who joined or rejoined the
Party after Germany invaded the Soviet Union. But this
view of leftists as nothing more than dupes or dopes and
of active Party members as the incarnation of evil does

not take into account the psychological and political effects of the long impotence of the democracies in con-
fronting Nazi aggression as the thirties wore on. Fascism
made Communists out of a fair number of otherwise intelligent people, who might simply have remained New
Dealers and incremental reformers had it not been for
Hitler. The idea that there must be an international, ideologically based resistance to fascism was the unifying
force. As Cooke noted in his book on the Hiss case:

> The one big nation that did not merely assist this
> view but had a whole philosophy about it was the
> Soviet Union. . . . Declared Communists could
> keep up the classic talk of a new order of society, of
> social justice and equality of economic opportunity;
> and—when you had no intimate acquaintance with
> how this paradise was being imposed on the people
> of Russia—it sounded just like the New Deal. Con-
> sequently, it didn't seem to matter much in the
> 1930s where a liberal left off and a fellow traveler
> began. . . . When the national governments of the
> democracies were helping Hitler to believe that
> there was no place they would put up a stand, no
> issue they would fight him on, the Soviet Union
> looked to many people like a tower of courage and

good sense with its straightforward appeal to all
anti-Fascists, all progressive movements, socialists,
and liberals, to join together and draw a line beyond which Hitler could be dared to go. It was un-
pleasant to be reminded in 1950 that, as the record
of the abortive French and British negotiations
with Moscow in 1939 showed, it was the Soviet
Union that had been ready to draw the line at
Czechoslovkia.[41]

One of the more notorious statements by left-wing intellectuals during this period came on August 26, 1939,
when, in a letter to the editor of the *Nation*, some three
hundred cultural figures denounced "the fantastic false-
hood that the USSR and totalitarian states are basically
alike." Among those signing the statement were Granville Hicks, Clifford Odets, Dashiell Hammett, S. J. Per-
elman, and James Thurber. The Nazi-Soviet pact was announced a week after the declaration was published.

Would Alger Hiss have signed such a declaration, had
he been a New York law school professor rather than a
government official? My guess is yes, but it is no more
than a guess. Would he have left the Party after the pact,
as Hicks and so many others did, or would he have tried
to justify the Nazi-Soviet alliance to himself? Assuming

that Hiss was a Party member in the late thirties (even if he was never Chambers's best Communist buddy), would he have been disturbed enough to quit after the Faustian Nazi-Soviet bargain was announced? Or would he have hung on until the United States entered the war on the side of the Soviet Union? Hiss does not even mention his reaction to the Nazi-Soviet pact in his brief account of his activities at the State Department. It was the pact, by the way, that impelled the remorseful ex-Communist Chambers to meet with Assistant Secretary of State Berle and name names (including Hiss's) of alleged Communists in the State Department. Chambers said he feared that the documents Hiss had turned over to Soviet agents would now wind up in the Reich Chancellery in Berlin. But Berle, as we know, did not follow up on Chambers's accusations in 1939. It would take nearly a decade, encompassing a world war, the emergence of the Soviet Union as a world power, and a sea change in American political passions, to put Chambers and Hiss, and their diametrically opposed stories, on public display in a courtroom. In the absence of that sea change, Chambers might have continued to rage, a Lear still trying to make himself heard above the indifferent wind, and Hiss might have finished his career as a faceless but influential bureaucrat. There would have been nothing iconographic about either man.

The Eye of the Hurricane, 1948–1950

On August 2, 1948, Whittaker Chambers appeared before the House Committee on Un-American Activities and named the names of several former government officials with whom he claimed to have been on intimate terms as a member of an underground Communist "apparatus" in Washington. One of those named was Alger Hiss. Chambers was subpoenaed by HUAC to corroborate the testimony of Elizabeth Bentley, a former schoolteacher who had named a great many names herself (though not Hiss's) and claimed to have been a courier between government officials and Soviet agents. Bentley, despite her willingness to name coconspirators, was exceedingly vague about the specific nature of the documents she had passed on. A spinster in an era when being an unmarried woman was even more disgraceful, in some quarters, than being a Communist, Bentley proved a perfect target for liberal satire. She claimed that she had made most of her espionage drops at all-American restaurants like Schrafft's and Howard Johnson's. "Never again," wrote A. J. Liebling, "after reading Miss Elizabeth T. Bentley's testimony . . . shall I think of the Schrafft's on Fifth Avenue near Forty-Sixth Street as an anodyne place, given over to the shopping luncheons of women from Connecticut and Westchester. Any outsize handbag in the joint may be packed full of what Miss Bentley called 'inside policy data,' written out on small slips of paper for delivery to a spy named Al."[1] It will doubtless be said that Liebling was a well-known fellow traveler and that his making fun of a forty-something aspiring drama queen was rather like former Vice President Dick Cheney taking aim at quail with clipped wings. Bentley's testimony wasn't enough for HUAC either, because there was no corroboration of her stories. One specific "secret" Bentley claimed to have revealed to the Russians was the approximate date of D-Day. In fact, independent accounts written by former army officers of unimpeachable security pedigrees (including one major general) indicated that our Russian ally had naturally been let in on the general time frame of the Normandy landing, scheduled for the last week in May or the first week in June 1944. HUAC hoped that Chambers would provide more concrete details to back up Bentley's story. At the beginning of the hearings, Chambers provided no details of spy operations; indeed, he initially testified that the Ware group of which he and Hiss were both members in Washington was *not* an espionage organization in the mid-1930s but was only—only!—a study group dedicated to infiltrating the government with communist sympathizers. The man from *Time* did, however, come up with a list of names that included Hiss's wife, Priscilla; his younger brother, Donald, a lawyer who had also served as Oliver Wendell Holmes's personal assistant and who had held minor administrative jobs in both the Agriculture and State Departments; and Lee Pressman, a Harvard Law School classmate of Hiss's and a former colleague at the Agricultural Adjustment Administration.

Of those named by Chambers, only Alger Hiss voluntarily offered to testify before HUAC to refute the accusation. It looked, at first, as if Hiss had made the right decision in showing up and aggressively defending himself. First, who but an innocent man would volunteer instead of waiting for a subpoena, flatly deny all of the accusations of having been a Communist, and refuse to take refuge in the Fifth Amendment? Second, Hiss's smooth and self-confident demeanor presented a sharp contrast to Chambers's unpolished performance. Even Richard Nixon, who had much more background about Hiss than the other HUAC members (though he concealed this knowledge from committee colleagues at the time) and who was already convinced that Hiss was lying, cited the effectiveness of Hiss's testimony. "Hiss's performance before the Committee was as brilliant as Chambers' had been lackluster," Nixon recalled. "The press section was crowded with newsmen, many of whom were acquainted with Hiss and had gained respect for the ability he had demonstrated as head of the Secretariat at the San Francisco Conference which set up the UN organization."[2] Everything about Hiss, including his easy relationship with the press, marked him as the kind of eastern establishment figure hated by Nixon all his life. The longtime *New York Times* correspondent and Nixonologist Tom Wicker reports that in one direct exchange, Hiss told Nixon, "I graduated from Harvard. I heard your school was Whittier."[3] Thirty years later, in a presidential memoir written in a much more statesmanlike voice than the agitated *Six Crises*, Nixon still could not resist revealing his detestation of Hiss's patrician manner. The former State Department aide had been much "too suave, too smooth, and too self-confident to be an entirely trustworthy witness."[4] Hiss appeared before HUAC to deny Chambers's accusations just three days later, on August 5, and—like Chambers's original charges—Hiss's denial was front-page news throughout the country. What followed, in swift succession, was the first face-to-face confrontation between the two men, in an executive session at the Commodore Hotel in New York; a televised public hearing (the first in American history) featuring the dueling testimonies of both men in Washington; Chambers's repetition on *Meet the Press* (a forum where interviewees, unlike witnesses at congressional hearings, did not enjoy immunity from libel and slander lawsuits) of charges that he and Hiss had been Communists together; Hiss's filing of a libel suit against Chambers; and a windup of the HUAC hearings with the realization that the ultimate judgment about who was lying (or who was telling the most important lies) would be made in courts of law and the court of public opinion. Representative J. Parnell Thomas of New Jersey, chairman of the committee, had opened the HUAC hearing by telling Hiss and Chambers that "certainly one of you will be tried for perjury."

What impression did the public have at the time, and how did people form their opinions? The Hiss affair was the last political drama in American history in which television exerted almost no influence. In 1948 fewer than 10 percent of American families owned television sets (compared with nearly half by the time of the Army-McCarthy hearings five years later, and 90 percent in 1960, when Nixon and Kennedy faced off in the first televised presidential debate). In 1948, however, people heard the news of the day on radio or read it in newspapers, and most papers—whether considered left, right, or centrist in their editorial views—gave the story front-page coverage from the first day Chambers leveled his charges. Bentley, whose testimony had also received front-page treatment, was frequently identified in headlines as the "Red Spy Queen." A Gallup Poll conducted two weeks after the Hiss-Chambers faceoff showed that nearly four out of five Americans had heard about the congressional spy hearings and that the same proportion wanted HUAC to continue its investigations. Three-quarters of Americans thought that there was "something to" the investigations, and only 17 percent dismissed the HUAC hearings as "just politics." Yet by the end of 1948, more than half of Americans still could not correctly explain the meaning of the phrase "Cold War." And in spite of the intense publicity surrounding the Hiss-Chambers confrontation, only 15 percent of those who could define the Cold War thought that Russia was "winning." Seventeen percent thought that the United States was winning, and 16 percent thought that neither country was winning.[5] In short, the American public, at the time when Chambers first leveled his charges against Hiss, was suspicious of Communists and concerned about Soviet influence in the world—but still not concerned enough to be paying close attention to the ins and outs of Cold War politics. The Hiss case, by virtue of the intense publicity surrounding both the HUAC hearings and the defendant's two trials for perjury, played a significant role in heightening public perceptions of danger from Communist subversion. The question is why Hiss? He was not the most important New Dealer named as a Communist or a fellow traveler by either Bentley or Chambers. Laughlin Currie, an economist and special assistant to Roosevelt, and Harry Dexter White, a former assistant treasury secretary who laid the foundation for the World Bank and became, in 1946, director of the International Monetary Fund, were much bigger fish than Hiss, who might best be described as an effective high-level administrator rather than a policy maker.* Hiss certainly did have access to classified

*White, who died of a heart attack just three days after testifying before HUAC, became a moot case; his friends, who included Alger Hiss, were convinced that the stress of the HUAC proceedings had killed White. He had vigorously denied ever having been a "fellow traveler" and noted that the Bill of Rights prohibits "star chamber proceedings." Information obtained from the Venona files in the 1990s does suggest that White was engaged in espionage.

documents in his administrative role as an aide to Assistant Secretary of State Francis B. Sayre, but he was not an influential Svengali, as he has often been portrayed, capable of changing the views of the president or the president's closet advisers. He was, however, in a position to copy documents that crossed his desk on their way to Sayre's office.

It is entirely possible that the Hiss case might have faded into history, like the cases of so many accused of being Communists, when the HUAC hearings, and their attendant surfeit of headlines, recessed in August as congressmen went home to campaign in an election year. Given Harry Truman's surprise victory in the November presidential election, and the shift from a Republican to a Democratic majority in Congress, it seems especially unlikely, in normal political circumstances and the normal course of legislative investigations, that HUAC would have continued its vigorous pursuit of a "he said, he said" dispute. But the circumstances and the twists of the case were anything but ordinary. On November 17 Chambers led congressional investigators to the soon-to-be-famous pumpkin-encased microfilm, containing copies of classified State Department documents, on his Maryland farm. The public knew nothing about the papers until, on December 3, HUAC's chief investigator, Robert Stripling, announced that the committee now possessed "definite proof of one of the most extensive espionage rings in the history of the United States"—copies of documents intended for transmission to Soviet agents. The following front-page headline in the *New York Times* typifies the most moderate approach of the press toward the sensational story:

HOUSE UNIT SEIZES
FILMED U.S. SECRETS
AT CHAMBERS' HOME

Vital State Department Data
Reportedly Fed to Red Spies
Bared in Row With Hiss

FEDERAL JURY MAY ACT

Committee Declares Evidence
Of Big Network is 'Definite'

Also in November, Chambers turned over stacks of typed copies of State Department documents, dated between

January and April 1938, dealing with subjects ranging from Hitler's plans for the annexation of Austria and the probable response of European governments to analyses of the Sino-Japanese War. These documents, Chambers charged, had been typed by Priscilla Hiss on the Hisses' Woodstock typewriter. (For those who know Woodstock only as a character in the comic strip *Peanuts* or as the site of a famous rock festival, the Woodstock typewriter was a subject of endless newspaper coverage and questions at both of Hiss's trials. Hiss's defenders maintained—and maintain to this day—that the FBI, or Chambers with FBI assistance, manufactured a copy of the Hisses' Woodstock in an attempt to frame the defendant.*

At first, public reaction from the liberal press and many Democrats was to pooh-pooh the importance of the documents themselves. As might be expected of any group of intragovernment communications, the pumpkin papers contained a good deal of bureaucratic dross, including the news that the Japanese government had tried to buy a manganese mine on a Costa Rican island where no manganese had ever been found and that the American consul

*For the most extensive discussion of the contents of the documents and microfilm, see chapter 7 of Weinstein's *Perjury*. The description of the contents, which is often extraordinarily vague in newspaper and magazine articles published between 1948 and Hiss's conviction in 1950, is precise in Weinstein's 1978 work.

general in Vienna had delivered the stunning prediction that "it seems possible Hitler is seeking a foreign political triumph at the expense of Austria."[6] Since this prediction was delivered just before the *Anschluss*, at a time when virtually every sentient European knew that Hitler was about to march into Austria, the real question was why we were paying a salary to a diplomat for purveying an opinion that could easily have been issued by anyone who read the daily papers in the United States, France, or England. But there were also many communications of much greater importance, in both the microfilm and the typed documents. These included a cable sent in code to the State Department from the American ambassador to France, William C. Bullitt, who was a close friend of the president. Sumner Welles, who was undersecretary of state during the period in which the documents were copied, testified that the Bullitt cable had been transmitted in one of the most secret codes used at the time, and that possession of the cable would have enabled a foreign government to break the American code. All of this, however, was beside the point if prosecution for espionage was the objective, because the statute of limitations on espionage had expired by the time Chambers led investigators to the pumpkin patch. Thus if Alger Hiss was indeed the conduit for the documents to Chambers, at a time when Chambers was still a Communist spy, both men could have been prosecuted for perjury.

Although there would have been no "Hiss case" without the pumpkin papers, Hiss's August testimony was enough to persuade many Americans, like my parents, that he was lying about his relationship with Chambers. In spite of a strong public distaste for former Communists who claimed to have seen the light and then turned on their old friends—a distaste that was still apparent at the voir dire for jurors before the first Hiss trial in 1949— Hiss's story about having forgotten that he once knew a man named George Crosley did not make sense to people unless they were already disposed to hate everything about the postwar anticommunist crusade. Hiss had gone out of his way to rent his accuser an apartment, lend him money, and give him a used car. Hiss's initial insistence that he did not recognize Chambers from his newspaper photographs after the first HUAC hearing also failed to ring true. Except for his grayer hair and cleaner teeth, Chambers did not look all that different in the late 1940s than he did in his pictures from the 1930s. One might easily forget the face of a cocktail-party acquaintance, but it is hard to forget the face of someone who borrows money and fails to pay it back. All of these quotidian matters, oddly absent from many of the books that devote hundreds of thousands of words to such Hiss esoterica as his hobby of bird-watching and the provenance of the Woodstock typewriter, may have had as much to do with convincing ordinary Americans that Hiss was lying as the documentary evidence.

Hiss's constant use (138 times, to be precise) of qualifying phrases like "to the best of my knowledge" and "to the best of my recollection" also gave the impression that he was a slick lawyer trying to leave himself wiggle room. And yet if Hiss sounded like someone with a strong motive for wanting to conceal past behavior that could ruin a career by 1948, Chambers sounded like, well, a nut. In his initial HUAC appearance, he testified that for a year after leaving the Party, he had slept only during the day, and had stayed awake at night with a gun at his side, for fear of being assassinated by Soviet agents. This testimony naturally raised the question of why, if Chambers was so terrified of Soviet retribution, he thought that it could not be exacted as easily by day as by night. At the later face-to-face confrontation, Chambers's teary-eyed claim that he had no personal motive for naming Hiss also made him sound slightly unbalanced or, at the very least, histrionic. When asked by the terrierish Nixon why he was turning on an old friend, Chambers rejected what he called a "story of an old grudge, of 'hatred' that has been going around." He emphatically declared, "I don't hate Mr. Hiss. We were close friends. But we got caught in the tragedy of history. Mr. Hiss represents the concealed enemy we are all fighting and I am fighting. I am testifying against him with remorse and pity. But in this moment of historical jeopardy, at which the nation now stands, so help me God, I could not do otherwise." Asked for his reaction to Hiss's testimony by committee member F. Edward Hébert, Chambers first replied flatly, "Mr. Hiss is lying." Hébert again asked, "You think his testimony is pure fabrication from whole cloth?" Chambers answered, "I'd say 80 percent fabrication." But psychologically troubled people may be telling the truth, just as paranoids may have real enemies. Reactions to the first confrontation at the HUAC hearings depended entirely on whether Chambers or Hiss made a more credible impression, because the drama took place before the statute of limitations on espionage expired and Chambers revealed his evidentiary ace in the pumpkin patch.

By today's standards, the progression from the revelation of the pumpkin papers in November 1948, to Hiss's conviction after his second trial on January 21, 1950, was remarkably swift, although the affair seemed to drag on forever to contemporary observers used to a stricter interpretation of a defendant's right to a speedy trial. A grand jury indicted Hiss on charges of perjury on December 15, 1948; the first trial began on June 1, 1949, and ended in a hung jury just five weeks later. The second and final trial began on November 17, 1949, and lasted just a few weeks longer, even though it was interrupted by the holidays. Public opinion, as indicated by Gallup Polls in which a large majority thought that HUAC should continue its hearings, was growing more favorable toward the investigators and less favorable toward anyone associated with communism. Even newspapers like the *New York Herald Tribune*, the *New York Times*, and the *Washington Post*—all of which provided balanced news coverage of the hearings and the trials—concluded that the Hiss-Chambers confrontation had justified the investigations of a committee theretofore regarded by liberal journalists with views ranging from skepticism to disdain. And, as Alistair Cooke noted, the very nature of the HUAC proceedings mimicked a trial and forced Hiss to provide a preliminary defense without any of the protections of a courtroom. Cooke observed that "the real mischief of a Congressional committee irresponsibly run amounts to this: that when it is investigating matters beyond the reach of the statute of limitations, it levels at suspect witnesses (by directly impugning their security and their good name) an oblique threat of attainder; and when it is investigating matters within the reach of the statute of limitations, it is directly usurping the function of the grand jury."[7] I well remember that my parents, in attempting to explain the Hiss case to me, referred to the HUAC hearings as "trials." Even so, the fact that half of those selected for the first jury pool had to be dismissed during voir dire because they doubted the veracity of ex-Communists showed that the public harbored significant doubts about Chambers as well as Hiss.

The case made by the prosecution at the first and second trials rested on roughly the same evidence—the microfilm from the pumpkin, copies of classified documents typed on the Woodstock machine once owned by the Hisses, and, above all, Chambers's testimony. Hiss's defense, too, rested on roughly the same premises at both trials—that Chambers was lying and that all of the documents at issue (and the typewriter) could have been the products of an elaborate forgery and frame-up. There was one significant addition to the defense case in the second trial—psychiatric testimony about Chambers's alleged psychopathic personality, which the first trial judge refused to allow but which the conservative Republican judge in the second proceeding, somewhat to the surprise of Hiss's lawyers, did admit into evidence. Judge Henry W. Goddard's admission of psychiatric testimony to impeach the government's prosecution witness set a precedent in federal cases, much as the great trial lawyer Clarence Darrow had in the 1920s, when he successfully introduced psychiatric evaluations to obtain life sentences rather than the death penalty for the convicted child-killers Richard Loeb and Nathan Leopold. But Leopold and Loeb were sentenced by a judge, whereas a jury was listening to the psychiatric analysis of Whittaker Chambers. In the 1940s and early 1950s, average Americans—unlike intellectuals who had embraced the religion of Freudian psychoanalysis—were not nearly as impressed by psychological expertise and authority as they would be two decades later. Belief in Freudian theory (and the defense witness, Dr. Carl Binger, like virtually all psychiatrists of his generation, was a thoroughgoing Freudian) was about as prevalent in the United States as belief in Marxism. In any event, the prosecution did an effective job of demonstrating that psychiatry was hardly an exact science—and that it probably would have been just as easy, had the government been so inclined, to produce a psychiatrist who would testify that Alger Hiss was a psychopathic personality. Binger, a well-known New York psychoanalyst, pointed out that Chambers avoided eye contact with his questioners and frequently looked at the ceiling—59 times, to be exact. This observation was offered in support of Chambers's "pathology." Binger also commented on Chambers's frequent use of the equivocal terms "it would have been" or "it should have been"—as opposed to "it was." As it happened, though, Binger's observations applied to Hiss much more than to Chambers. While Chambers used these conditional, equivocal expressions only 10 times in his testimony, Hiss used them 158 times, according to the official transcript. Binger stuck to his testimony that Chambers was psychopathic, while admitting that other psychiatrists might come to different conclusions. Hiding the papers in the pumpkin was just one piece of evidence of this psychopathology. Normal people, Binger said soberly, keep important papers in banks. The prosecutor countered by asking the good doctor whether Moses's mother had not hidden him in the bullrushes. "She could scarcely have put him in a safe-deposit box," Binger replied. This use of psychiatric testimony, however innovative, may have been a big mistake on the part of Hiss's defense team—not only because jurors at midcentury were still unaccustomed to the use of "mental health professionals" as hired guns but also because the murky and pseudoscientific nature of the testimony—right down to analyses of Chambers's expressions that were directly contradicted by the trial transcript—was evident to anyone paying close attention. Using psychiatry to attack Chambers may well have struck the jury as just one more damning piece of evidence of Hiss's arrogance and elite class status. The *Nation's* Robert Bendiner, who covered both of Hiss's trials, provided one of the most enterprising inquiries into the value of such psychiatric testimony by talking with several analysts about their colleague's attempt to impeach Chambers. Two of the psychiatrists interviewed by Bendiner (unnamed, because the time had not yet arrived when every ambitious shrink would aspire to the high-profile public image of Dr. Phil) scoffed at the idea that a proper medical diagnoses could be made without any personal contact with the "patient." One of these psychiatrists told Bendiner that "a psychopathic personality . . . may be a troublemaker, but he may also be a superior person." Being a psychopathic personality "has in itself no bearing whatever on his capacity as a witness, since such persons may just as well be over-meticulous about telling the truth as given to chronic lying." By the same token, a pathological liar might be perfectly sane—or at the very least, not qualify for any legal definition of insanity. From a third psychiatrist (also anonymous), Bendiner received a different opinion. "This doctor felt that the case marked an advance for both psychiatry and the law, inasmuch as it recognized the need for professional aid in dealing not merely with 'legal insanity' but with irrational motivations of behavior that fall short of the psychotic."[8]

At the beginning of Hiss's first trial, Bendiner observed that if Hiss were to be found innocent, the verdict would "prove the undoing of the House Committee on Un-American Activities; that body would stand revealed as a collection of gulls who for two years had followed the lead of a man regarded by a jury of average Americans as a monumental liar or mental case." Hiss's conviction, by contrast, would demonstrate "that Communist conspiracy has gone much farther in the United States than the run of liberals have thought possible."[9] Of course, Hiss's conviction demonstrated no such thing to a great many liberals, who continued to believe that he had been the victim of a witch hunt—and that no elaborate deception was beyond the FBI and right-wing Republicans in their hunt for Communists. The reaction of both the left-wing and the right-wing press was entirely predictable. "We told you so" was the basic line of the political right, but it is impossible to believe that the minds of conservatives like William F. Buckley, Jr., would have been changed had Hiss been acquitted—any more than the minds of liberals were changed by the guilty verdict. It took a quarter of a century, by which time Weinstein had used the Freedom of Information Act to force the government to release much more documentation than had been available at the time of the trial, for many liberals to come to the reluctant conclusion that Hiss had indeed been a Communist spy.

Editorials published in the nation's leading newspapers in the days and weeks following Hiss's conviction for perjury offer considerable insight into the passionately held views that formed the iconography of the case at the time and would continue to influence public opinion throughout the McCarthy era. Newspapers, it must be emphasized again, were the chief sources of public information about the case. Anyone who doubts that the hunt for American Communists was also an attack on the New Deal need only read the explicit indictment of the Truman and Roosevelt administrations in the conservative *Chicago Tribune.* "So we find this traitor hobnobbing through the years with the mightiest of the New Deal mighty," the *Tribune* editorial intoned. "He advises the President. He is the favored protégé of two men who are kingmakers within the burocracy.* One of them, Felix Frankfurter, is a man who moves the members of his personal entourage into ever greater posts of power and

---

*The phonetic transliteration of certain words like *bureaucracy* into *burocracy* was a trademark of the *Tribune* at the time. I spent the first eight years of my life in Chicago, and until my second-grade teacher in a parochial school—the nuns were sticklers for correct spelling—taught us about diphthongs, I had been convinced by the *Tribune* that *through* was spelled *thru.*

influence. He is the patron saint of Hiss." The editorial
concluded that while only one man, Hiss, had been convicted, "the guilt is collective" and "spreads over the New
Deal, which sponsored and protected this monstrous
conspiracy against America."[10] In the *Washington Post*, a
centrist-liberal paper in a company town, the editorial
consensus was that Hiss was guilty but that if Republican
legislators used the verdict "to drag the case into the political arena, they will do a disservice to the whole Nation." Adopting much the same tone as Alistair Cooke
would in his book on the case, the *Post* argued that Hiss
"had the misfortune of being tempted to betray his country in an era of widespread illusions about communism
and of being tried for perjury in connection with his
offense in a period of cold war when the pendulum of
public sentiment had swung far in the other direction."
The *Post*'s contention that "no generalized conclusions
can be drawn from the fact that one official has proved
unfaithful" seems mordantly hilarious in retrospect,
given that it took Joe McCarthy only two weeks to level
the charge of extensive Communist infiltration of the
State Department. "Nothing could please the Kremlin
more than to see Americans tearing their society apart in
an internal feud," the editorial warned.[11] If that was true,
the Kremlin certainly got its wish. (Twenty years later,

when I was a working journalist and the wife of the *Washington Post* correspondent in Moscow, we were constantly treated to spurious comparisons between McCarthyism and Stalinism by members of the Soviet "official intelligentsia" permitted to associate with foreigners. Many of these Russians were well-educated writers and journalists with close ties to the KGB, and they knew perfectly well that there was no comparison between McCarthy, who was brought down by the very constitutional protections he had assaulted, and Stalin, who was responsible for the murders of millions and could be brought down only by his own death.) For centrist American liberals during the McCarthy years, the idea that we were actually helping Soviet Communism by using constitutionally dubious and socially disruptive methods to track down American Communists was to become a standard argument—and the Hiss case played an important role in framing that argument because so many liberals for so long believed him innocent. Indeed, Hiss used the same argument himself in later years—but the premise worked for him only because he continued to maintain that he had never been a Communist.

The editorial assessment of Hiss's conviction in the *New York Times* was brief (unlike most other newspaper editorial commentary), and its tone was one of sorrow and sympathy rather than anger. "Few of those who have followed Mr. Hiss's career from its early and brilliant beginnings can be insensitive to the pathos and tragedy of this outcome," the editorial declared. Hiss was an intelligent and educated man "who seemed a man of high purpose. He had many friends, eminent and otherwise, who continued to have faith in him. It is difficult to understand the motives or the reasoning that might have led him into association with Mr. Chambers in acts harmful to his own country." It was not difficult, of course, if one accepted that Hiss had indeed been a member of the Party. In conclusion, the editorial said that Hiss had received a "full and fair" trial and that his lawyers had been given an even fuller opportunity in the second trial than in the first to marshal any evidence that could exonerate the defendant of the government's charges.[12] The responses of readers to this editorial were and are extraordinarily revealing, because they encapsulate all of the conflicting views that have kept the Hiss case alive among political intellectuals for the past half-century. "Is the nation mourning the conviction of Alger Hiss?" asked one man from Davenport, New York. "One would think so from your editorial, 'Mr. Hiss Found Guilty.'" The letter writer maintained that the "average American knows the 'cold war' represents, not an accidental international situ-

ation but a well-outlined plan dating back to war and prewar days and agreements made by his own Government."
Another citizen, by contrast, took the *Times* to task for its
statement that Hiss had been given wide opportunity to
exonerate himself. "In the American system of justice a
defendant is not supposed to be required to exonerate
himself of a government accusation," the letter said. "He
is entitled to be presumed innocent until his guilt is
proved beyond a reasonable doubt. . . . We are fond of referring to the New England witch trials of the seventeenth century without remembering just what was
wrong with those trials. Their flaw was not the charge; if
one believes in witches it is perfectly reasonable to accuse
a person of being one. The flaw is that people were executed because they could not exonerate themselves by
proving that they were not witches."[13]

Arthur Miller would cover the same ground in *The
Crucible* in 1953, as would right-wingers who replied that
the difference between the postwar hunt for Communists
and the Salem witch trials was that there were no witches,
while there really were American Communists. But there
is no denying the genuine role of communism, anticommunism, witchcraft, and the effort to persecute witches in
American intellectual and religious history. There certainly were people in the seventeenth century who not

only believed in witchcraft but who regarded themselves or their enemies as witches. That most of us do not believe in witchcraft today has nothing to do with the damage to the colonial social fabric inflicted by those who sought to uncover and eliminate witches in their midst. If one concedes the existence of both self-defined witches and real Communists, that still does not answer the question of how bad these people were and what damage they inflicted on American society. The fundamental political disagreement over the answer to that question is surely the main reason why the Hiss case refuses to go away.

THREE

Competing Narratives and Public Amnesia, 1950–1965

In the closing days of the 1952 presidential campaign, Republican vice presidential candidate Richard Nixon launched a direct attack on the Democratic presidential nominee, Adlai Stevenson, for having testified as a character witness on behalf of Alger Hiss at his first trial. Stevenson, who had known Hiss briefly in 1933 when they were both young New Deal lawyers at the Agricultural Adjustment Administration, had testified that Hiss's reputation was "good." In a nationwide television broadcast, Nixon concluded that Stevenson's "actions, his statements, his record disqualify him from leading . . . the fight against Communism at home and abroad." The Republicans were in a tricky position in regard to "the Hiss issue," because Dwight Eisenhower's chief foreign policy adviser, John Foster Dulles (who would become secretary of state in the new Republican administration), had supported Hiss's selection as president of the Carnegie Endowment and was elected chairman of the endowment's board at the same meeting at which Hiss's appointment was confirmed. Dulles eventually became a witness for the prosecution against Hiss, although he acknowledged under cross-examination that Hiss's reputation had been "very good" at the time he was tapped for the prestigious Carnegie post. Nixon, in another hard-hitting speech on the weekend before the election, said the difference between Dulles and Stevenson was that Dulles had changed his mind about Hiss. (The term *flip-flop* had not yet become a cliché in political discourse.) "Mr. Stevenson has never expressed one word of indignation at Alger Hiss's treachery," Nixon thundered. "Like [former Secretary of State] Dean Acheson, he says he does not question the legal verdict. But, also like Acheson, to this day he has not 'turned his back on Alger Hiss.'" Nixon was referring to Acheson's statement, issued at a press conference, that he had known Hiss and his brother since childhood. "I think that every person who has known Alger Hiss or has served with him at any time has upon his conscience the very serious task of deciding what his attitude is and what his conduct should be," Acheson told reporters on January 25, 1950. "For me, there is very little doubt about those standards and those principles. I think they were stated for us a very long time ago. They were stated on the Mount of Olives." Neither Acheson's allusion to the New Testament nor his suggestion that old friends do not abandon one another in time of trouble made a favorable public impression at the time; to carry the biblical allusion one step further, Acheson was crucified in the right-wing press for his position. Not surprisingly, Whittaker Chambers's former employer, *Time*, declared that the Republicans were getting the better of the Democrats in the argument over the Hiss case and the larger issue of "softness on Communism." *Time* was undoubtedly right in its evaluation of public opinion, but it is unlikely that either a general fear of domestic communism or the specifics of the Hiss case played a decisive or even a significant role in Eisenhower's overwhelming electoral victory. Among those who voted for Eisenhower, corruption in government was cited by 42 percent as their major concern, followed by the Korean War (24 percent) and communism in government as a distant third (just 9 percent).[1] Eisenhower's promise to go to Korea in an effort to bring about an end to the war, coupled with the fact that whenever he smiled, people immediately felt better about everything,

would undoubtedly have carried the day without any last-
minute dredging up of the Hiss case by Nixon. Nevertheless, the Hiss case remained a touchstone of Cold War
passions even though he had been in prison since 1950.
Julius and Ethel Rosenberg, convicted of atomic spying
and sentenced to death in 1951, were on death row await-
ing the results of their appeals. There were undoubtedly
many anticommunist crusaders who thought that death
row was exactly where Hiss also belonged. He was "the
one who got away," the symbol, to those who still believed the government was filled with traitors, of the
faintheartedness of the United States in combating its
deadly enemy.

Serving his sentence in the federal penitentiary at
Lewisburg, Pennsylvania, and deprived of any public
forum, Hiss was considered a convicted traitor rather
than merely a convicted perjurer by the public. He had no
way to tell his side of the story; most of the fire still surrounding his case was stoked by the 1952 publication of
Chambers's autobiography, an instant bestseller written
with such emotional conviction that it is hard to put
down even today, when history has contradicted many of
the author's political judgments—chief among them the
conviction that communism was going to win the battle
for hearts and minds around the world. (One wonders

what the born-again Chambers would have though of radical Islamism as an alternative organizing principle to communism.) Chambers was absolutely convinced that he had chosen the losing side in his break with the Communist Party and that Hiss, even though he was in prison, had chosen the winning side. When Chambers began to think about quitting the Party in 1937, he told his wife, "You know, we are leaving the winning world for the losing world." This conviction was a true indicator of the permanent ideological power of the Party over susceptible individuals; even as Chambers rejected the idea of communism, he still could not conceive of a world in which the Soviets might lose out to more democratic societies. The "witness" still believed, in the early fifties, that Soviet-style communism was going to take over nation after nation and insisted that "nothing has changed my determination to act as if I were wrong—if only because, in the last instance, men must act on what they believe right, not on what they believe probable." He then made the choice "to die, if necessary, rather than to live under Communism."[2]

Chambers describes both his conversion to and his abandonment of communism in religious terms. As he watched his baby daughter in her high chair, he was overcome by belief in a phenomenon that would be called intelligent design by antievolutionists today. "I was watching her eat," Chambers recalled. "She was the most miraculous thing that had ever happened in my life. . . . My eye came to rest on the delicate convolution of her ear—those intricate, perfect ears. The thought passed through my mind: 'No, those ears were not created by any chance coming together of atoms in nature (the Communist view). They could have been created only by immense design.'" (These awe-inspiring revelations were visited upon Chambers at the same time that he was still engaging in homosexual one-night stands up and down the East Coast—a fact that he had revealed to the FBI but did not include in *Witness*.) And Chambers recognized the religious nature of both his communist and postcommunist faith, noting, "I had not changed from secular to religious faith in order to tolerate a formless good will vaguely tinctured with rationalized theology and social uplift. I was not seeking ethics; I was seeking God. My need was to be a practicing Christian in the same sense that I had been a practicing Communist."[3] Small wonder that the imprisoned Hiss, reading excerpts serialized in the *Saturday Evening Post*, wrote his wife that *Witness* was "clearly the product of a disturbed psyche."[4] No one, apart from Hiss's family, was thinking much about him after the penitentiary doors slammed shut. The McCarthy era was at its height, but most of the articles written about the Hiss case in the early fifties were responses to *Witness*. G. Edward White points out in *Alger Hiss's Looking-Glass Wars* that only five essays about the Hiss case were published in major literary journals between 1950 and 1952. All were written by anti-Communist liberals who had been fellow travelers or Party members in the thirties. These included Leslie Fiedler, Granville Hicks, Sidney Hook, Arthur Koestler, and Diana Trilling.

One of the most perceptive analyses of *Witness* was written by the philosopher, ex-Marxist, and anti-Communist liberal Hook, who did not attempt to plumb the depths of Chambers's psyche but observed that most Americans in 1952 were unlikely to approach the book with any objectivity because their minds were already made up about the Hiss case. Writing in the *New York Times Book Review*, Hook made a sharp distinction between what he considered the internally consistent facts of the autobiography— Chambers's account of the Hiss case and the psychology of communists—and Chambers's interpretation of the facts, which placed the blame squarely on atheism and equated nearly all liberals with communists. Hook foreshadowed the arguments over the line between dissent and disloyalty that have added fuel to the culture wars since the 1960s:

The view that man must worship either God or
Stalin faces many formidable theoretical difficulties
and has the most mischievous practical consequences. . . . There exists a not inconsiderable body
of men who worship both. . . . After all, religious
faiths have been compatible with the most diverse
social principles. Not a single policy about empiri-
cal arrangements in human life can be logically
derived from transcendental religious premises
or from propositions of rational theology. . . .

Indeed, Chambers has reflected poorly about the
facts of his own disillusionment with communism.
He writes dramatically of the "screams" of the victims of communism, of the shattering effect of
these messages from souls in torment, on even
hardened Communists. He is silent about the fact
that the truth about the Moscow trials . . . was first
proclaimed by liberals like John Dewey. While
Chambers still worked for Stalin's underground,
it was *they* who sought to arouse the world to the
painful knowledge he is now frantically urging
on it. . . .

It is unfortunate that Chambers could not have
given a wiser and more generous expression to his
faith. The logic by which he now classifies liberals

and humanists with the Communists is not unlike
the logic by which, when a Communist, he classified them with Fascists. . . . I should hope that
Chambers himself would recoil from the implica-
tions of his present view that there is no loyal political opposition outside the Faith. When heresy is
identified with the enemy, we shall have seen the
end of democracy.[5]

It is hardly surprising, in view of the fact that Hiss was in
prison for the first half of the decade, that the focus of
public attention remained on Chambers. It is somewhat
more surprising that Hiss did not attract more attention
after he was released from jail, launched his lifelong campaign for vindication, and published his own account of
the case, *In the Court of Public Opinion*, in 1957. The problem was that Hiss's memoir is arguably the dullest book
ever written about the Hiss case. It is devoid of political or
social analysis, not to mention emotion. Nearly the entire
text is devoted to a precise, point-by-point effort to refute
all of the circumstantial evidence presented in the case—
especially the expert testimony upholding the prosecution's contention that many of the government documents were copied on a Woodstock typewriter owned by
the Hisses. Hiss's tedious style put off even those entirely

convinced of his innocence. "The documents admittedly typed by the Hisses on the machine owned by them in the early 1930s," Hiss reports dutifully, "were typed on a machine previously owned by Mr. Thomas Fansler, father of Mrs. Hiss. The available evidence points to the fact that this machine was in use in Mr. Fansler's office at least as early as July 8, 1929, and therefore could not have been the typewriter now in possession of the defense . . . "[6]

Only the most dedicated Hissophile or Hissophobe could follow such minutiae, then or now. This is particularly true because Hiss persists in referring to himself and his wife in the third person; a few references to "Priscilla and I"—as opposed to "the Hisses" would have gone a long way toward humanizing the author and making the story more intelligible. In the *Nation* after Hiss's conviction, Robert Bendiner observed that to believe Hiss had been framed, one must accept the assumption that "Chambers had long ago plotted to destroy Hiss, for some reason which the defense chose not to speculate on in court, and that through the years he spun the web. He made it his business to find out what the interior of the Hiss homes looked like, down to the last detail, and communicated the facts to his wife for future testimony; he learned the dates and amounts of Hiss's withdrawals from the bank, the dates of his vacations, and so forth."[7] That is in fact what many of Bendiner's colleagues at the *Nation* did believe. Bendiner's articles, however, were models of fairness—even as McCarthy's charges were justifying the worst fears of liberals about the effect of the Hiss case on civil liberties.

The argument that Chambers had engineered a long-term conspiracy against his former friend made no more sense to most Americans in 1957, when Hiss published his version of the case, than it had seven years earlier. But another, more powerful factor was working against Hiss in the early stages of his campaign for rehabilitation: Americans, with the exception of committed liberal and conservative intellectuals, were simply not as interested in the issues of domestic communism or Communists in government as they had been during the early fifties. Had Chambers waited as long to tell his story as Hiss did, the public might not have been any more interested in *Witness* than it proved to be in Hiss's legalistic brief on behalf of his innocence. Ironically, the widespread conviction that Hiss was a traitor coexisted with a growing public indifference to the very issues that, only yesterday, had impelled newspapers to describe Hiss's prosecution as "the trial of the century." Hiss himself was already yesterday's news.

Intellectuals on both the left and the right, because of their own ideological preoccupations, have tended to exaggerate the anticommunism of the general public during the late fifties. White, for example, argues that a major factor in the widespread acceptance of Hiss's status as a convicted traitor was "the recoil of American intellectuals from Soviet Communism, and the resultant collapse, in the community of persons who regarded themselves as political 'progressives' or 'liberals' of any sympathy for the popular front 'collectivism' of the 1930s." For former Communists as well as fellow travelers, the "only hope for respectability was to follow Chambers's path, that of open renunciation of their former pro-Soviet sympathies and vigorous engagement with anti-Communism."[8] Respectability to whom? White seems to be suggesting here that there was no honorable course for anyone who had once been attracted to communism *except* to "follow Chambers's path" and name names. But there were many intellectuals who had no use for Soviet Communism by the fifties and nonetheless refused to pass harsh retrospective judgment on those who had held different opinions in the thirties. One was Arthur Miller, who observed in his 1977 autobiography *Timebends* that "as in Salem, a point arrived, in the late forties, when the rules of social intercourse quite suddenly changed, or were changed, and attitudes that had been merely anticapitalist-antiestablishment were now made unholy, morally repulsive, if not actually treasonous then implicitly so. America has always been a religious country."[9] Miller had never been a Party member, but like so many intellectuals of his generation, he counted many former Communists among his acquaintances. Called to testify before HUAC in 1956, he refused to take the Fifth Amendment but also refused to talk about anything but his own political activities and opinions—in other words, he refused to name names. But the fall of Joe McCarthy had dampened public enthusiasm for the much of the anticommunist crusade—especially when presided over by politicians—and although Miller was convicted of contempt of Congress, his stance did not make him a pariah. (His 1957 conviction was overturned on appeal.) Even as he was being cited for contempt of Congress, *The Crucible*—which was greeted with mixed reviews and lasted six months on Broadway in 1953—was already becoming more respected and respectable. Within a few years after Miller's citation for contempt of Congress, the play would be required reading in many high school English classes. Miller may not have been respectable by the standards of *Partisan Review* and *Commentary*, but he soon became respectable enough for American theater audiences and school boards. Moreover, as the fifties turned into the sixties, there was a renewal of the American distaste for informers that had

been apparent in the voir dire before the first Hiss trial—
and a heightened respect for those who, like Miller, had
refused to take the Fifth Amendment in order to avoid
being punished for their unwillingness to label old friends
as onetime Communists.

By 1959 communism had actually dropped off the Gallup
list of the most important problems facing the nation.
"Keeping the peace" was listed as the no. 1 problem by 38
percent, followed by the high cost of living, the struggle
over racial integration, and unemployment. This does
not mean that Americans were unconcerned about possible military threats from the Soviets, but it does mean
that they also had other priorities, such as control of
atomic weapons. In the late fifties, ordinary Americans
began to worry about whether an atomic war might not
start by accident rather than by the perfidy of the Soviets.
These concerns would soon to be addressed in popular
movies like *On the Beach* (1961), *Fail-Safe* (1964), and the
iconoclastic comedy *Dr. Strangelove* (1964). *On the Beach*
was based on Nevil Shute's 1957 novel, portraying a
world in which every human being is being destroyed by
radiation but no one can remember who started the war

or why. *Fail-Safe*, adapted from a bestselling 1962 novel, featured a memorable performance by Henry Fonda as an American president who deliberately drops an atomic bomb on New York after Americans have accidentally bombed Moscow. The sacrifice of New York is seen by both the president and the Soviet premier as the only way to prevent all-out retaliation and a subsequent world war. In one poignant scene, the American president asks his interpreter if he knows the biblical story of the sacrifice of Abraham. The Soviet leader is portrayed as being every bit as sorrowful as his American counterpart about the necessity of such a choice—a depiction that would have been unthinkable in an American movie a decade earlier. *Dr. Strangelove*, Stanley Kubrick's savage, satirical version of the *Fail-Safe* scenario, depicted military hawks on both sides as lunatics. Right-wingers hated these movies, with their emphasis on the possibility of human error and lunacy rather than the evil of one side; the point is not that the plots were credible but that for many Americans, the films about doomsday scenarios raised questions that were taken seriously. Many social commentators talk about "the fifties" and "the sixties" as though they were entirely distinct cultural decades, but the second half of the fifties and the first half of the sixties had more in common culturally than either had with the more fearful, conformist early fifties or with the socially turbulent second half of the sixties.

It was still too soon, however, for Alger Hiss, even if his book had been more frank and persuasive, to make any progress at rehabilitating himself in the court of public opinion. The growing public detachment from the Cold War iconography of the early fifties did not change many people's minds about Hiss's guilt; it simply rendered the entire affair more remote. Hiss's first job offer after prison came in 1957, from the president of a company called Feathercombs, Inc. Andy Smith, the company's founder, read a profile of Hiss in the *Times Book Review*, which revealed that Hiss was looking for a job. Smith had little interest in Hiss's past; he simply saw the chance to hire a No. 2 man, one who desperately needed a job, for $5,000 instead of the $20,000 salary he had expected to pay. A convicted perjurer proved to be a bargain hire for a small company. In an article published in *Esquire* magazine in 1960, Brock Brower reported on the American public's short memory span. Hiss, whose picture had once been on every front page, was rarely recognized by customers and business associates during his years at Feathercombs. "Haven't I met you someplace before?" salesmen would ask when introduced to Hiss. Occasionally, he was confused with the Nazi Rudolf Hess.[10]

On the rare occasions when he was invited to speak in public, Hiss bored his audiences with the dry, impersonal generalizations and the legal pedantry that had made his book a commercial failure. Describing the audience response to a lecture that created enormous controversy (before the event) at Princeton, Brower writes that "the plain fact is that they were bored—to some extent because the lurid expectations had been frustrated, but also because the lecture was dull and uninformative. All this tells heavily against Hiss. Even his well-wishers came away disappointed, troubled by a vague feeling that the man must be disingenuous if he appears that blank in public." Hiss never seems capable of getting beyond "his own pedantic manner," Brower added, noting that during the trials, Hiss had been impelled "to make the blunder of correcting prosecutor Thomas Murphy's grammar from the witness stand."[11]

Even though the time was not yet ripe for a full public reconsideration of Hiss's claim of innocence, it is clear from his activities during the outwardly unfruitful decade after his release from prison that he never lost sight of his ultimate goal of exoneration. His determination to publish a book about his case was a significant factor in his separation from his wife, Priscilla. According to many scholars and the Hisses' son, Tony, Priscilla Hiss objected strongly to the reopening of the old wounds of the trial. Without doing just that, Hiss could never obtain the vindication he sought.

One important element in the drive to regain his reputation was the active social life Hiss maintained in New York, among old friends and supporters as well as new acquaintances. Brower reported that Hiss was considered "quite a social catch" by New York hosts and hostesses. "People are astonishingly anxious to make his acquaintance nowadays," Brower noted,

> and if there is some cuteness about it at first ("Alger Hiss! Oh, I'm dying to meet him!"), his relations with people quickly find firmer ground and often, though cautiously on his part, lead to new friendships. At a first meeting with someone, he has a way of immediately seizing on the other person's interests, following these up in casual chitchat until he's had more time to size up his man. If satisfied, he moves on to more personal give-and-take. People find him "charming," "a wonderful conversationalist," "mentally impeccable" "not bitter, not cynical," "a nice, comfortable person" with a "sweetness about him."[12]

This passage bears a strong resemblance to one of Whittaker Chambers's descriptions of his relationship with

Hiss. "The outstanding fact about Alger Hiss," Chambers recalled, "was an unvarying mildness, a deep considerateness and gracious patience that seemed proof against any of the ordinary exasperations of work and fatigue or the annoyances of family or personal relations."[13] There was, of course, nothing astonishing about the desire of New York intellectuals, journalists, publishers, lawyers, socialites, and social climbers to meet Hiss. He already had many friends and acquaintances in the worlds of journalism and publishing, not yet lumped together as "the media," during his first life before the HUAC hearings and his perjury conviction. The renewal and expansion of these contacts during his early years in New York would prove exceedingly useful to Hiss in the future, when many Americans would begin to view Cold War assumptions more skeptically. During this fallow period in the late fifties, Hiss developed another relationship that would further his long-term goal of public vindication. He agreed, uncharacteristically, to extensive interviews with a psychiatrist, Meyer Zeligs, for a book Zeligs planned to write on the psychological aspects of the Hiss case. The book, *Friendship and Fratricide: An Analysis of Whittaker Chambers and Alger Hiss*, would be published in 1967, and Zeligs was able to do for Hiss what Hiss was never able to do for himself: he presented Hiss as a multidimensional human being rather than as a cool manipulator. In Zeligs's book, the story of Hiss's reaction to the suicides of his father and, later, his older sister, was publicly told for the first time, and told in much greater detail than Hiss would reveal in his own memoir twenty years later. Although Hiss and his relatives cooperated with Zeligs, Chambers (who died in 1961) and his relatives did not. In *Friendship and Fratricide*, Hiss would emerge as a man who had risen above the traumas of his personal life to become an outstanding contributor to society, while Chambers would be portrayed, much as he had been by the psychiatrist Carl Binger at the second trial, as a sociopath. The only difference was that Zeligs was free to speculate about what had been concealed at trial—Chambers's homosexual past. And Zeligs focused on Chambers's supposed homoerotic feelings for his older brother, Richard, who had committed suicide by sticking his head in an oven in 1926. In Zeligs's scenario, Chambers had transferred his homoerotic feelings for his brother to Hiss—*Et voilà!*, we have the motive for Chambers's framing of the unattainable man who aroused his deepest yearnings. That Hiss would agree to be interviewed for such a book—even while he publicly maintained a posture of being above all personal emotional revelation as a tool for gaining public sympathy—seems to be yet another sign of his ability to compartmentalize his life or, more accurately, lives.

As the fifties turned into the sixties, Hiss parted company with Feathercombs and began earning his living as a stationery salesman. Brower found it ironic that Hiss, with a formidable résumé that might once have ended with a federal judgeship or a much higher post in the State Department, had been reduced to "that most mundane of American goals, and the last one that anybody would think that Alger Hiss would end up in pursuit of: a customer."[14] Yet one of the consistent themes of Hiss's life, beginning with the Old Boy teas at Felix Frankfurter's home, was his ability to charm people and tell them what they wanted to hear—the essential trait of a good salesman. Is there any more recognizable icon in American culture than that of the salesman? How can a "sweet," "comfortable" man, having survived a legal ordeal without succumbing to bitterness or cynicism, be lying when he maintains that his ordeal was a politically motivated, base pursuit of someone too innocent and too decent to imagine that he might not be believed?

FOUR

The Best of Times, The Worst of Times, 1970–1980

At the height of the Watergate scandal in July 1973, the *New York Times* published an op-ed piece, titled "My Six Parallels," by Alger Hiss. The headline was, of course, an allusion to Richard Nixon's *Six Crises*, and Hiss's short essay explicitly compares the conduct of the HUAC investigators at his own hearings with the illegal tactics used by Nixon's henchmen against Democrats and opponents of the Vietnam War. The appearance of Hiss's byline in such a prominent mainstream forum was one indicator of how far he had come, since the days when he could only get jobs selling hair accessories and stationery, in his campaign to restore his public reputation. One of Hiss's parallels was "forgery by typewriter," which Hiss had always considered the linchpin of the government's case against him. During Watergate, one of the White House "plumbers," E. Howard Hunt, admitted to having forged a document to aid the Nixon administration's vendetta against Daniel Ellsberg, who was responsible for making the Pentagon papers public in 1971.* Another of Hiss's parallels was the use of a principal witness who was an "unstable informer" in the 1972 trial of a group of antiwar activists known as the Harrisburg Seven. The best-known defendant was the Reverend Philip Berrigan, who was already serving a sentence in the Lewisburg penitentiary (the same institution where Hiss had been incarcerated in the fifties) for destroying Selective Service records. The informer in the Harrisburg case was Boyd Douglas, Jr., an ex-convict who had done time in Lewisburg for passing bad checks and had "befriended" his fellow prisoner Berrigan. Berrigan and his codefendants were charged with conspiracy to kidnap Henry Kissinger

*Ellsberg, a Southeast Asian expert and an analyst for the Rand Corporation, had a top-level security clearance and was responsible for leaking documents, known as the Pentagon papers, about government deception in support of the Vietnam War. The Pentagon papers were published in the *Times* in 1971, after the Nixon administration was rebuked by the Supreme Court in its efforts to suppress the material. Ellsberg expected to be tried and convicted for releasing classified information. He was not prosecuted, however, because of the accumulation of evidence that the government had engaged in grave and unconstitutional misconduct in its pursuit of him. Among other activities, the White House plumbers had broken into the office of Ellsberg's psychiatrist.

and blow up steam tunnels under government buildings. The trial ended in a hung jury in 1972, and the Nixon Justice Department, hobbled by the expanding Watergate scandal, did not refile charges. This was one of many cases in the late 1960s and early 1970s in which juries refused to convict defendants on vague conspiracy charges—especially if the main evidence was provided by an informer. "In my case," Hiss reminded *Times* readers, "Whittaker Chambers had a similar record as an admitted perjurer and could have been indicted at the pleasure of the Department of Justice. A young Congressman, Richard M. Nixon, publicly opposed the indictment of Chambers on the ground that it would destroy the case against me."[1] Nixon's involvement in both controversies was the biggest parallel of all.

There is no way to overestimate the importance of Nixon himself in the improvement of Hiss's public image in the late sixties and early seventies. Long before Nixon's election, though, the social changes of the sixties had generated much more sympathy for all who their/lost jobs, reputations, and personal freedom during the McCarthy era. The seventies were, for the most part, a decade of counternarratives, challenging the Cold War assumptions that had led the United States into the Vietnam War and portraying the hunt for domestic Communists after the Second World War not only as a threat to American civil liberties but also as a fundamental misjudgment and exaggeration of the importance of communist influence within the nation. These counternarratives included both scholarly studies, such as David Caute's *The Great Fear* (1976), and personal memoirs, such as Jessica Mitford's *A Fine Old Conflict* (1978), a witty, if somewhat historically obtuse, account of her life as a member of the American Communist Party from the Second World War through the late fifties, when Nikita Khrushchev denounced Stalin's atrocities and nearly every American with a functioning brain quit the Party. Mitford is surely right in her contention that many Americans joined the Party not because they wanted to betray their country but because they wanted to work for social change. But she is quite blind about the extent to which membership in the Party induced even its most intelligent members to ignore evidence. In 1955 Mitford and her husband visited Hungary and experienced "general euphoria" about the improvements in the lives of workers and peasants under Communist rule. When a waiter asked them to mail a letter to his brother in the United States, they asked, "Is there some problem about mailing letters out?" Although the man "was evidently in real distress," Mitford acknowledges, "we regretfully decided we could not perform his

mission; what if he was a spy, an opponent of the government?" At the time, Mitford saw no contradiction between her husband's activities as a lawyer fiercely defending the civil liberties of American Communists and her
assumption that an opponent of the government should
have no rights in a Communist paradise. The following
year, of course, Hungarians revolted and the uprising was
put down by the Red Army's tanks. Mitford notes, in a
whopping understatement, that "one thing was dismally
clear: on our visit to Hungary . . . Bob and I had entirely
failed to perceive the widespread discontent that must
have seethed beneath the surface."[2] The reviews of Mitford's book, except from the far right, celebrated the wit
of the author of *The American Way of Death* (1961) and ig-
nored the evidence Mitford provides about the capacity
of the Party to corrode the political judgment of members who loudly, and rightly, denounced their own government for much milder actions to suppress dissent than
those routinely practiced in Communist states.

In the early seventies, Hiss had been able to make
progress, particularly among intellectuals, in reshaping
the image of a convicted liar and traitor into that of someone who had been the victim of ethically tainted, oppor-
tunistic Communist-hunters like Nixon. Not that the
Hiss case was in the forefront of anyone's mind in a coun-

try still being torn apart by the Vietnam War, but as the sixties turned into the seventies, large numbers of Americans (sometimes for opposing reasons) became much more suspicious of government itself, and much more aware of abuses of power by agencies like the FBI, than they had been in the fifties and early sixties. For one thing, J. Edgar Hoover himself, who presided over the FBI until his death in 1972, was no longer a sacrosanct figure. His efforts to undermine the civil rights movement by implying that it was a Communist plot—and that Martin Luther King, if not actually a Communist himself, was nothing more than a fellow traveler—had met with success only among hard-core segregationists. Blackmailable politicians were still terrified of Hoover, but his name—and the image of the incorruptible "G-Man"—was no longer a totemic invocation of American righteousness. By the late sixties, it had become almost impossible to recall that Democrats like Harry Truman, just twenty years earlier, had frequently appealed to the FBI as a barrier against the excesses of politicians who sat on committees like HUAC.

The rise of the New Left also prepared the ground for Hiss's renascence—but not, I think, for the reasons generally cited by historians and social critics on either the left or the right. G. Edward White argues that Hiss benefited from the rise of the New Left because "a new generation of students could suddenly identify with the heady reformist spirit of the young New Dealers."[3] I find this an incredible assertion, which only proves that serious people of every generation continue to look at the same "facts" and reach entirely different conclusions about the reasons for the durability of the Hiss controversy. White and I are near-contemporaries; I was twenty-five in 1970, the year in which he graduated from Harvard Law School. I had been an education reporter for the *Washington Post* during the previous five years, when the escalation of the Vietnam War fueled student uprisings on campuses across the country. To me, the most striking thing about the New Left on college campuses by the end of the sixties was its ahistoricism. I would be extremely surprised if the Hiss case meant anything at all to the majority of the students, born after 1945, who occupied college buildings and shut down campuses between 1967 and 1971. Perhaps students at Harvard Law School were better educated than most of those I interviewed, and that accounts for White's conviction that the popularity of the New Deal with a new generation had something to do with Hiss's improved stature. Certainly the historical memories of Hiss, Felix Frankfurter, and Oliver Wendell Holmes, Jr., not to mention many other Harvard Law

School graduates called to testify before HUAC, may have been stronger in Harvard Yard than they were among most Americans or on most college campuses. And Alger Hiss was a better-known figure to the older leaders of the New Left—those born in the late 1930s and early 1940s— than to student protesters too young to have any first-hand memories of the McCarthy era. Indeed, some of the early members and founders of Students for a Democratic Society (SDS) were Red Diaper babies, the children of former Communists, and they had good reason to take the Hiss case personally. Hiss and Bob Dylan were both enthusiastically received when they showed up to check out the proceedings at a 1963 meeting of SDS organizers, most from the preboomer generation, but Hiss receives almost no attention in the extensive memoirs by early participants in and founders of this significant organization. (Hiss receives exactly two lines, for instance, in Todd Gitlin's detailed memoir, *The Sixties: Years of Hope, Days of Rage.* Gitlin, born in 1943, was present at the SDS committee meeting visited by both Hiss and Dylan. He notes only that Hiss received a round of applause, while he talks about the excitement generated by Dylan for many pages.)

Furthermore, the New Deal meant almost nothing to the children of the baby boom (which, according to demographers, began in 1946), to whom, by the end of the sixties, the social struggles of the thirties seemed as remote as the American Revolution or the Civil War. As a reporter, I was struck by the sense that a majority of activists in the New Left—and the younger they were, the more strongly my generalization applies—had no confidence at all in the ability of government to effect any positive social changes. Some were openly contemptuous even of the reformist spirit, a real descendant of the New Deal, that inspired the passage of Medicare, civil rights laws, and the war on poverty during the early years of Lyndon Johnson's administration. For the college-age baby boomers, the escalation of the war in Vietnam had completely obliterated the early accomplishments of a president whose views on domestic policy were formed during the New Deal era.

The greatest support for Hiss, and the real explanation for his new cachet on campuses as the sixties turned into the seventies, was generated not by nostalgia for the New Deal on the part of students but by memories of the McCarthy era ingrained in many faculty members. University communities had been disproportionately affected by the anticommunist investigations of the late forties and early fifties because academics, like writers and artists, were more likely than other Americans to have been

drawn to leftist (though not necessarily Communist) politics in the thirties. Middle-aged faculty members—some
of whose lives had been directly affected by the hunt for
Reds—were strongly inclined to believe that Hiss had
been framed. By world historical standards, the repres-
sion of the McCarthy era was relatively contained. Only
two people, Julius and Ethel Rosenberg, were executed.
Hundreds were jailed, and thousands more lost their jobs.
As David Caute notes in *The Great Fear* (1978), "In
France, Italy, and Germany, the blood flowed; in Britain
and America, mainly tears." Those tears, however, were
particularly common in intellectual communities and
professions—teaching among them—that were particular targets of the Red-hunters of the fifties. A teacher's
taking the Fifth Amendment at federal or state legislative
hearings was generally considered more than sufficient
grounds for dismissal. Professors at taxpayer-funded state
universities were especially vulnerable. In California,
where the state legislature was particularly aggressive in
pursuing former Communists, the University of California simply capitulated in 1952 to a demand by the state's
Un-American Activities Committee that a former FBI or
military intelligence agent be placed on every campus to
investigate the faculty.[4] At Michigan State University in
the early sixties, I was taught by a number of middle-aged

professors who had themselves been fired by other universities during the McCarthy era: they wound up, gratefully, at Michigan State because its president, John A. Hannah, was a strong-minded liberal Republican who disliked McCarthyism and who possessed enough political power of his own to shield the faculty from fishing expeditions by a state legislature that would have liked to expose as many pinko professors as possible. Michigan State had another advantage in avoiding the attention of the state legislature. The University of Michigan at Ann Arbor, the premiere public higher education institution in the state, had a much "pinker" reputation—which it justified as the fifties turned into the sixties by providing a significant number of leaders for the newly organized SDS. One was Tom Hayden, in 1960 editor of the student newspaper, the *Michigan Daily*. Indeed, the first nationally publicized SDS conference, titled "Human Rights in the North," was held in Ann Arbor in 1960 and brought together young activists like Hayden with older civil rights activists like Bayard Rustin and Michael Harrington.

The main attraction of Hiss for the New Left was not his New Deal past but his adversarial past in relation to Richard Nixon. By the early 1970s, when Hiss was being invited to speak on many more campuses than he had been in the 1960s, liberal academia's dark memory of Mc-

Carthyism fused with anger at contemporary government attempts to suppress antiwar activism: Tricky Dick
was the bad actor who linked the two eras. In the minds of
many middle-aged liberals (including those who never
had any use for Soviet or Chinese Communism), the violations of constitutional liberties that came to be known
as Watergate, employed this time to further the nation's
involvement in Vietnam, were an extension of the Mc-
Carthyite abuses of the past. Hiss fitted into the picture
not only because many on the left saw him as a victim of
Cold War hysteria but because he also stood for—had always stood for—a multilateral foreign policy rather than
the unilateral exercise of American power that had drawn
the nation deeper and deeper into an unwinnable war in
Southeast Asia. Although Hiss was sometimes asked to
talk about the New Deal in university settings, his real
appeal was to those who saw the Vietnam War as a logical
outgrowth of the long-term Cold War blinders that had
drawn the United States first into Korea, then, in 1962,
into a near-lethal confrontation with the Soviet Union
over missiles in Cuba, and finally into Vietnam. Many in
his audiences could see no distinction between Ellsberg,
who revealed the Pentagon papers to the world, and Hiss,
who, if he had handed over copies of government documents to the Soviets (the crime with which he was never

charged), was often excused by liberals on grounds that he had spied, if he did spy, for higher antifascist ends. The obvious difference was that Ellsberg never attempted to evade the consequences of his actions. Nevertheless, if you considered Ellsberg a hero rather than a traitor, as I and so many of my contemporaries did, it was easier to give Hiss a pass even if you thought, as I did, that there was something fishy about his story. Furthermore, Hiss deliberately associated himself with the antiwar movement—a major departure from his avoidance of overt, public political activities in the early sixties. During the trial of the Harrisburg Seven, he joined more prominent opponents of the war, such as the Reverend William Sloane Coffin and Bella Abzug, in speaking outside the Pennsylvania courthouse where the defendants were being tried. On campuses, Hiss frequently spoke about the Yalta Conference, the United Nations, American foreign policy in the Far East, the McCarthy era, and the press's role in fanning anticommunist flames. By the mid-seventies, we were no longer a people who unquestioningly subscribed to John F. Kennedy's dictum that we must "pay any price, bear any burden, meet any hardship, support any friend, oppose any foe to assure the survival and success of liberty"—not, at any rate, if assuring that success meant intervening in a seemingly endless civil war thousands of miles from home. "I didn't include my own case as a separate topic," Hiss would recall, "but it usually came up as a matter of course, and I always answered questions about it from my audiences."[5] Of course the case came up, and of course Hiss took every opportunity to tell his version of the truth to sympathetic audiences disposed to believe that anyone who had run afoul of Nixon must, by definition, be a pretty nice guy and a straight shooter. It enraged conservatives that Hiss, formally convicted of perjury and considered guilty of spying in the fifties' "court of public opinion," was viewed by the mid-seventies as a respectable expert on foreign policy by a large portion of the academic community.

For those whose political consciousness was formed during the closing years of the Vietnam War and the Watergate era, it was easy to believe that the government of the United States was capable of doing almost anything in an effort to portray dissenters as traitors. Marxist, socialist, and small-c communist thought did not seem threatening to those of us who (unlike most of the New Left radicals) were still proud to call ourselves liberals. We certainly had no illusions about Soviet Communism; the Soviet tanks that rolled through the streets of Prague in 1968, smashing the Czech reformist movement promoting "socialism with a human face," had erased any atavistic sentimentality about the heirs of the Bolsheviks. But we were also believers in the need for capitalism with a more human face and for the development of an international system that could mediate the disputes of the world's great powers without war. Hiss, as a spokesman for the older generation of internationalists, seemed, at the time, to be more a man of the present and the future than the past—not a relic of the New Deal but someone who had been ahead of his time. By the mid-1970s, when Hiss was also in his seventies, he was seen by a younger generation, which did not know much about the facts of his case, in very much the same light as his near-contemporary, Dr. Benjamin Spock—as an opponent of the war and a strong critic of Nixon. Had Hiss been a Communist? Well, a lot of people had been Communists in the thirties and had since come to their senses. It was certainly possible to have been both a Communist and a victim of political persecution. The federal courts, much more liberal as a result of eight years of appointments not only by Kennedy and Johnson but by the unpredictable Nixon, took an increasingly dim view of governmental actions that tried to skirt the Bill of

Rights.* In 1972 the Supreme Court overturned the 1954 "Hiss Act," which denied government pensions to any employee convicted of perjury in a case involving national security. The 1954 law had been specifically designed to deny benefits to Hiss, who had been a federal employee for nearly sixteen years before he left to become president of the Carnegie Endowment. In 1975 Hiss's license to practice law in Massachusetts, automatically revoked when he became a convicted felon, was restored. In a somewhat astonishing decision, given the absence of new evidence, the Massachusetts Supreme Judicial Court ruled that "fairness and fundamental justice demand that the person who believes he is innocent though convicted should not be required to confess guilt to a criminal act he honestly believes he did not commit."[6] During this period, Hiss was frequently described in the public prints, and privately by his many friends, as "optimistic" about his own future and the future of his country. And why not? As early as 1972 Hiss told an in-

---

*Nixon appointed two Supreme Court justices, Harry Blackmun and Lewis F. Powell, who would become reliable members of a pro–civil liberties high court for the next two decades. Although Nixon undoubtedly had no idea of just how liberal and libertarian Blackmun and Powell would become, he tended to appoint judges with moderate Republican backgrounds—that is, judges who were not "strict constructionists" as the term is understood by the Republican right today.

terviewer that "by the time I am 80, I expect to be respected and venerated."[7]

Hiss never achieved his goal of attaining general respect,
veneration, and public vindication. Even in the mid-seventies, when Hiss was most lionized by the academic left
and the entire McCarthy era was being reexamined not
only in academia but in popular culture, Hiss's cause was
not anyone's first choice as an illustration, for widespread
public scrutiny, of the evils of anticommunist zealotry.
One of the most popular movies of 1973 was *The Way We
Were* (who can forget the "misty water-colored memories" of the movie's infernally ubiquitous theme song?),
starring Barbra Streisand and Robert Redford as star-
crossed lovers eventually torn apart by her pinko past and
their disagreement about the case of the Hollywood Ten.
(In the movie's final scene, the divorced characters meet
again, somewhere in the mid-1950s, in front of the Plaza
Hotel in New York. Streisand's character, still a model of
political virtue, is handing out ban-the-bomb leaflets,
while Redford, who once aspired to be a novelist, has sold

out to write for television.) In 1976 came *The Front*, a more serious satirical look, directed by Martin Ritt and starring Woody Allen and Zero Mostel, at the way blacklisted Hollywood screenwriters managed to make a living, writing anonymously for the movies and television. Even then, there were too many unanswered questions surrounding the Hiss case to sustain either a piece of sentimental kitsch like *The Way We Were* or a pointed comedy. If, by the early seventies, Chambers looked like a monochromatic villain to many on the left, in and out of the movie business, that did not make an ideal hero out of Hiss.

But the first real blow to Hiss's ambitions for general public vindication—as distinct from the respect he enjoyed among many scholars and writers on the left— came in 1978, with the publication of Allen Weinstein's *Perjury*. The book, at least nine years in the making, was a major publishing event at a time when the release of serious books—even those unsuited to be made into movies— could still be described as major publishing events. *Perjury* influenced a great many liberals who had never quite made up their minds about the Hiss case, and it elicited a skillful counterattack from Hiss's defenders, chief among them Victor Navasky, who had just become the editor of the *Nation.** Weinstein, then a professor of history at Smith College, presented himself as an objective scholar who, at the beginning of his quest for the truth about the Hiss case, thought that both Chambers and Hiss had lied—Hiss about the extent of his relationship with Chambers and Chambers about Hiss having been a Communist spy. This posture always seemed to me somewhat disingenuous on Weinstein's part, for the obvious reason that there would have been no particular motive for Hiss to have lied about how well he knew Chambers if they had *not* shared a Communist past. The possibility that Hiss lied about knowing Chambers leads inevitably to the possibility that Hiss was lying about everything else. Nevertheless, Weinstein had Hiss's full cooperation in the early years of the project, even before, backed up by the American Civil Liberties Union, he sued for the re-

---

*I should say, for the record, that I once had a slight social acquaintanceship with Allen Weinstein, who, in the late 1960s, was a close friend of my best friend's fiancé. I have no idea what he thought about the Hiss case at the time, or indeed whether he thought about it at all. My only impression of him was that he was an extremely ambitious young academic, and I was not surprised, a decade later, to find that he had chosen a subject for a big book that was bound to make a splash. I also know Victor Navasky, on a slight social as well as a professional basis, and I consider him one of the great editors of our time, even though I have not always agreed with his political judgments. I mention these personal connections not because they have any real bearing on my own evaluation of the place of Alger Hiss in American history but because they attest to the fact that almost no one in the worlds of journalism or historical scholarship (no one over fifty, at any rate) can claim more than a few degrees of separation from the heavyweight battlers in the Hiss arena.

lease of thousands of pages of FBI files on the case. As Weinstein tells the story in his book, he was already beginning to change his mind about Hiss as a result of his interviews with people who knew either Hiss or Chambers. Weinstein even traveled to Hungary to track down J. Peters, the Soviet agent described by Chambers in *Witness*. Yet Hiss must certainly have believed that Weinstein's research was going to support his claims of innocence, or he would not have agreed to be interviewed in the first place. Exactly why Hiss was so convinced that Weinstein would exonerate him is unclear. As Navasky noted in 1978, "a review of [Weinstein's] previous writings reveals no commitment to the innocence of Alger Hiss."[8] In an article in the *American Scholar* in 1971—in which he called for the FBI files to be made public—all Weinstein really said was that he did not believe there was enough evidence to support the conclusion that Hiss had been a Communist or a spy for the Soviet Union. But that was apparently enough to convince Hiss of Weinstein's objective bona fides. Five years and thousands of FBI documents later, Weinstein had his final meeting with Hiss, which he later described in an interview with the writer Philip Nobile. Weinstein told Hiss that he originally thought "that you had been far more truthful than Chambers. But after interviewing scores of people, looking at the FBI files, finding new evidence in private hands, and reading all of your defense files, every important question that existed in my mind about Chambers's veracity has been resolved." Weinstein concluded: "I don't think you'll believe me, but I want you to know how hard this has been for me and how terrible I feel that what emerges now may cause various of your friends, whom I have gotten to know as individuals, additional suffering." According to Weinstein, Hiss looked at him and asked contemptuously, "You really believe this is going to make me suffer?" By 1978 Hiss reportedly described Weinstein as "a small-time college professor from a small college" who was "trying to get to the big time through me."[9] (Nobile was one of the many journalists who believed in Hiss's innocence at that time. In 1976 Nobile lunched with Hiss and found that he "elicited sympathy and trust." Surely, Nobile wrote, Hiss could not be the "kind of monster [who] would compromise his family and friends" in service to a lie.)[10]

Although there was no "smoking gun" in Weinstein's book, he did turn up the new evidence that supported Chambers's rather than Hiss's story. The FBI and State Department files, which Hiss had always maintained would show that the government had suppressed exculpatory evidence, did no such thing. Equally important were interviews with old associates of Chambers (including Peters, who was unquestionably a Soviet agent), refuting the theory, long advanced by Hiss's defenders, that Chambers had been fantasizing about his own past as a Communist spy as well as about Hiss's activities. The contention that Chambers was too disordered a personality to have been recruited for espionage rests on the naïve premise that spies must be meticulous and effective and that the people who hire them must possess a fair amount of acumen. This delusion about the intelligence of those who engage in secret intelligence work seems to appeal to a fair number of liberals as well as conservatives. Of course, spies who are bumbling crackpots are probably capable of doing as much damage to the interests of one nation or another—albeit a different kind of damage—as those who are accomplished at their profession. Weinstein was careful not to claim that his research proved Hiss guilty of spying beyond a reasonable doubt—a reservation largely unshared by the many reviewers who implied that *Perjury* had indeed produced a smoking gun. In his concluding sentence, Weinstein states simply that "the body of available evidence proves that he [Hiss] did in fact perjure himself when describing his secret dealings with Chambers, so that the jurors in the second trial made no mistake in finding Alger Hiss guilty as charged."[11] In a

review in the *New York Times*, Christopher Lehmann-
Haupt observed that "it is now Hiss who appears inexpli-
cable and Chambers whose every move seems understandable and consistent with his character. It is now
Chambers who apparently can rest on his reputation
(however controversial it may remain) and Hiss whose
burden it is to dispel the aura of mystery."[12] *Perjury* certainly did change the minds of many liberals who had
theretofore considered themselves "agnostics" on the
question of Hiss's guilt or innocence, although I suspect
that some of these people were convinced not by the book
itself but by its glowing reviews. Weinstein's 674-page
tome, like nearly every other study of the Hiss case except
Cooke's 1950 book, presents a dense narrative that is ex-
cruciatingly difficult to follow. (This may be one of the
main reasons why no one every made a major movie out
of the Hiss case.) Who definitely had the Woodstock
typewriter in his possession on what date? How good a
typist was "Prossy" (Priscilla Hiss)? Was Chambers invited to the Hiss home under the name of George Crosley or did he simply "drop in?" Did Chambers eventually
go to the dentist because Hiss told him his teeth needed
work? Or would he have sought dental help anyway, once
he got a job with health benefits at *Time*? But it was this
very doggedness, and the accumulation of detail, that

made Weinstein's work more persuasive than the many
earlier books in which the authors were clearly on either
Hiss's or Chambers's side right from the start. The appearance of bias—often an outright admission of bias—
was much more striking in other books about the case,
from the dark anti-Hiss *Seeds of Treason* (1950), by Ralph
de Toledano and Victor Lasky (whimsically dedicated to
"Joseph Stalin, without whose help this book would never
have been written") to the pro-Hiss *Alger Hiss: His True
Story* (1976), by the journalist John Chabot Smith. The
Smith book, published just two years before *Perjury*, was
reviewed negatively by none other than Weinstein in the
New York Review of Books. Writing at what was arguably
the high point of Hiss's comeback, Smith failed to turn
the tables against the Hiss-doubters and place them on
the defensive. Weinstein's book, by contrast, would succeed in placing Hiss's die-hard defenders on the defensive. Nevertheless, the indefatigable Navasky managed to
find a number of flaws in Weinstein's scholarship—particularly regarding the Woodstock typewriter—and published them in a lengthy article in the *Nation* only a week
before *Perjury* began to receive major reviews. Thus reviewers like Lehmann-Haupt were forced to take into account the errors Navasky found. One of Navasky's most
telling points was his citation of several specific instances

in which the "corroborative evidence" Weinstein offered for Chambers's testimony was originally provided by Chambers himself to other historians. Thus Lehmann-Haupt concluded with a caveat:

> In the April 8 issue of The Nation magazine . . . Navasky . . . raises serious questions about Mr. Weinstein's objectivity and backs them up with at least a dozen major examples of Mr. Weinstein's distortion of the record he has unearthed. . . . As Mr. Navasky himself concludes, these apparent flaws in "Perjury" do not by themselves prove that Hiss is innocent. They only suggest that Professor Weinstein, like other commentators he himself assails for partisanship, has somewhere along the line been seduced into factiousness. Instead of finally settling an ideological battle that has been fought intermittently for 30 years now, "Perjury" appears to be just another incident in the war.[13]

Lehmann-Haupt was wrong. The publication and reception of *Perjury* may more accurately be compared to a major battle, which—although it did not produce an unconditional surrender—left the other side to fight a guerrilla war with vastly inferior resources. Weinstein's book is generally described as the "definitive"—the word was used in many obituaries of Hiss in 1996—work on the case. Those who still do not consider Hiss's guilt an established truth are generally regarded, as Navasky notes, with the same respect accorded those who still believe that the sun revolves around the earth.[14] In much the same spirit as evolutionary biologists who refuse to debate creationists, Weinstein generally turns down all invitations to appear in public forums with those who remain unconvinced of Hiss's guilt "beyond a reasonable doubt." To consider the case debatable today is to place oneself outside mainstream scholarly and political discourse. I elicit reactions ranging from pity to contempt when I tell conservative acquaintances that although I certainly agree that Hiss was guilty, I also think that undermining the legacy of the New Deal was a major goal of the anticommunist crusaders after the Second World War—as it remains a persistent goal of the political right today. To understand how and why Hiss's guilt remains so important to the right—and why questioning his guilt remains so important to a small and shrinking segment of the left, it is as critical to reexamine the rise of the New Right in the 1980s as it is to scrutinize the politics of the Old Left of the thirties and the New Left of the sixties.

The Rise of the Right and the Cold War at Twilight, 1980–1992

Ronald Wilson Reagan, the fortieth president of the United States, was, as is well known, a liberal Democrat and a supporter of the New Deal during the 1930s. He was thirty-seven years old in 1948, when Whittaker Chambers launched his spectacular charges against Alger Hiss, and the future president was among the majority of Americans who concluded that Hiss was lying. The Hiss case marked a turning point in Reagan's political loyalties, and in 1952 he supported the Eisenhower-Nixon ticket. Reagan considered Chambers a true hero and described his story as representative of "a generation's disenchantment with statism and its return to eternal truths and fundamental values." In a 1984 speech at his alma mater, Eureka College, Reagan referred reverentially to Chambers's description in *Witness* of the religious epiphany he experienced at the sight of his daughter's ear. The president said that Chambers's courage in breaking with communism had ushered in a "counterrevolution of the intellectuals." That counterrevolution, Reagan suggested, was irreversible.

> For most of my adult life, the intelligentsia has been entranced and enamored with the idea of state power, the notion that enough centralized authority concentrated in the hands of the rightminded people can reform mankind and usher in a brave new world. Well, I remember hearing one commonly held view of the Roosevelt era that all societies were moving toward some form of communism.
>
> Well, we know now that the trend in America and the democracies has been just the other way. In the political world, the cult of the state is dying; so, too, the romance of the intellectual with state power is over.[1]

Reagan's use of the word *intelligentsia* to describe left-wing intellectuals "enamored with the idea of state power" was (and is) a peculiar locution of right-wing political

speech. The term *intelligentsia* originated in prerevolutionary Russia and had almost never been used in the
United States, but right-wing ideologues since the early
1980s have used it to associate liberal intellectuals with
something that sounds vaguely un-American and alien. In
Russian, as the Oxford English Dictionary correctly
notes, the word originally meant the "part of a nation . . .
that aspires to intellectual activity; the class of society regarded as possessing culture and political initiative."*

Earlier in 1984, when Reagan awarded the Presidential
Medal of Freedom posthumously to Chambers, he most
certainly did not describe the man he was honoring as a
member of the intelligentsia (although he would undoubtedly have placed Hiss in that category). Reagan's
award to Chambers was a move that Richard Nixon, because of his personal involvement in the case, would never
have dared to make. The following year, Reagan paid
tribute to Chambers again at a party celebrating the fifti-
eth anniversary of *National Review* (where Chambers had

---

*During the Soviet era, the "engineers of human souls," as Stalin described
writers, broadened the definition; official newspapers used such terms as *techni-
cal intelligentsia* (meaning anyone from a real engineer to a designer of plumbing
fixtures) and *creative intelligentsia* (artists, composers, literary figures). I never
heard any Russian use such terms in private, as distinct from public and political, speech. Political dissidents spoke only of the difference between the *official
intelligentsia*—meaning lapdogs designated by the Party) and the *real intelligentsia* (meaning roughly what it meant in prerevolutionary Russia).

been a staff member in the late 1950s after leaving *Time*). In 1963 Richard Hofstadter noted that American intellectuals, certainly in the twentieth century, have historically been identified with liberalism. When William F. Buckley, Jr., founded *National Review*, he and a handful of other conservatives represented a tiny minority among intellectuals, and they had little political influence. That began to change in the late sixties, when the term *neoconservative* began to be used to describe intellectuals who had once identified themselves as liberals and had changed their minds. Many of the neoconservatives were Jews who had always been anticommunist but had taken a liberal stance on domestic social issues in the past. In the late sixties and even more markedly in the seventies, the neoconservatives embraced many other tenets of political and cultural conservatism, from lower taxes for the rich to an alliance with the emerging Christian Right.

Anticommunism, powerful as it was, became only one element in neoconservative thought. Norman Podhoretz, the editor of *Commentary* (whom Reagan specifically praised in his Eureka speech), turned what was then the flagship magazine of the American Jewish Committee—and a publication that had, in the past, included many political points of view—into the voice of neoconservatism. But neoconservatives really came into their own politically when Reagan began running for the presidency. Here, at last, was a jovial conservative candidate who, unlike Nixon, was actually liked by ordinary Americans. And just as John F. Kennedy had turned to the liberal intellectuals of academia to serve his administration, Reagan turned to conservative intellectuals who had not, before 1980, had a real taste of power.

The intellectual architects of the Iraq war during the administration of President George W. Bush—including Paul Wolfowitz, Richard Perle, William Kristol, and Elliott Abrams—cut their teeth during Reagan's two terms of office in the 1980s. Wolfowitz and Perle both worked in the Department of Defense during the Reagan years, while Kristol was an adviser to the archconservative Secretary of Education William Bennett. Abrams, who became Bush's deputy national security adviser for "global democracy strategy," was assistant secretary of state for Latin American affairs during Reagan's second term and had played a major role in the promotion of American military support for the Nicaraguan Contras. Convicted on charges related to the Iran-Contra affair, Abrams was pardoned by President George H. W. Bush in 1992, which left him free to return to the government payroll when the younger Bush entered the Oval Office—a testament to conservative family values in action. The presence of an influential group of right-wing intellectuals, moving seamlessly from right-wing think tanks and foundations to the administration of like-minded presidents, was something that liberal intellectuals, based mainly in academia, did not envisage in the 1970s.

In the eighties, the rise of the right—and the proliferation of people in government who not only celebrated the Cold War but revered the ex-Communists who had informed on their former comrades—spelled more trouble for Hiss's rehabilitation campaign. The young conservatives who filled so many important jobs in the Reagan administration believed in old Cold War verities and took Hiss's guilt for granted; the sort of speechwriters who inserted the word *intelligentsia* into Reagan's speech succeeded in mainstreaming what had once been considered right-wing political ideas. Furthermore, the disappearance of Nixon from the public stage, and the inevitable fading of public memories of the Watergate era, meant that the general intellectual community, regardless of its political values, was somewhat less interested than it had been in the seventies in a man who had played a leading role in a distant Cold War drama. Hiss was still invited to lecture on campuses, but his audiences were smaller than they had been in the seventies.

In the courts, Hiss lost a long battle for the granting of

a *coram nobis* petition, a rarely successful legal strategy in which a conviction is vacated because of errors of fact creating manifest unfairness in the original trial. Since the approval of a *coram nobis* request amounts to a complete overturning of a jury verdict, the standard of proof for the petitioner is extremely high. (In some cases, courts have even refused to approve such petitions based on the availability of DNA evidence that did not exist at the time of the original trial.) In 1983 the Supreme Court upheld the rulings of lower federal courts and put an end to Hiss's legal efforts.

Yet the conservative turn of American politics in the eighties did not further erode Hiss's support among those who had remained convinced of his innocence (or, at the very least, unconvinced of his guilt) after reading Weinstein. Indeed, the ascendancy of unapologetic intellectual as well as political conservatism at the highest levels of government, coupled with Reagan's inclusion of Chambers in the right-wing pantheon, may have had the opposite effect: liberals who had strong doubts about Hiss were once again reminded of everything that disgusted them about the prosecutorial right-wing anticommunism of the forties and fifties. In a 1986 article for the Sunday magazine of the *Washington Post*, David Remnick (a former Moscow correspondent for the *Post* and now editor of the *New Yorker*) emphasized the ambiguity surrounding both the case and Hiss's personality. "Even the most ardent partisans on either side sense the ambiguity," Remnick wrote. I remember reading Remnick's piece with particular interest, because some of Hiss's comments startled me. When Remnick mentioned that the "democratic socialist" Irving Howe was now convinced that Hiss had lied, Hiss replied acidly, "Howe? Howe? I don't consider him to be on the left." Asked if he admired Stalin, Hiss replied, "Oh yes. In spite of knowing the extent of his crimes, he was very impressive . . . decisive, soft-spoken, very clear-headed. He spoke almost always without notes." This struck me as a genuinely bizarre observation for anyone to make in 1986, by which time there was a huge amount of accumulated evidence—supplied not only by such outspoken opponents of Soviet Communism as Aleksandr Solzhenitsyn but by dissident Soviet Marxist historians like Roy Medvedev—that Stalin's rule had been not only brutal but utterly inefficient, a disaster for the Soviet economy from almost every standpoint as well as a disaster for human rights. Saying that Stalin spoke without notes was about as meaningful as praising Hitler for vegetarianism. Hiss would repeat and expand on his irrelevant musings about Stalin's good qualities—the gracious host at Yalta!—in his *Recollections of a Life*. Hiss's comment about Howe, however, is the observation most indicative of a Communist background. Real, pro-Stalin Communists in the thirties genuinely hated socialists and other kinds of liberals, because they offered an alternative on the left to the Bolsheviks; for whatever reason, Hiss's mask slipped when Remnick mentioned Howe, and he made the rare mistake of displaying genuine anger instead of maintaining a superior posture of tolerance. But the passage in Remnick's article that made me most dislike Hiss was his self-righteous insistence that he pay for his own lunch. "I insist on making this lunch dutch," he declared with a combination of pomposity and bonhomie. "That was the way with us New Dealers. We paid our own way."[2] This quotation perfectly captures the manipulative side of Hiss. He pays for his own lunch; ergo he must be incorruptible. Does letting someone else buy you lunch mean that you are going to lie? It is impossible not to recall the cafeteria lunch, described by Chambers in *Witness*, at which he claimed to have first met Hiss. Presumably, everyone paid his own check. Perhaps if I had ever met Hiss, I would have been as charmed by him—the word *charming* comes up repeatedly in maga-

zine and newspaper profiles—as most of the other writers
who spent time with him without buying him a meal.

One phenomenon of the eighties that ran counter to the
conservative political script—a development that certainly belied the predictions of Reagan's hero Chambers
—was the rise of Mikhail Gorbachev in the Soviet Union.
The emergence of a genuine reformer from within the
ranks of the Soviet *nomenklatura* was a possibility that had
never really been envisaged by conservatives or liberals in
the United States—including most scholars who had
devoted a lifetime to studying Soviet affairs. Most of
the hard-right intellectuals praised so highly by Reagan
thought that Gorbachev was a phony and dismissed his
calls for a new openness (glasnost) in Soviet society and
for a fundamental rebuilding (perestroika) of the com-
mand economy as public relations ploys designed to lull
the suspicions of a fundamentally anticommunist administration. There was only one problem from a right-wing
perspective: Reagan seemed inclined to give Gorbachev
the benefit of the doubt. He was eager to meet with the
new Soviet leader—Gorbachev became general secretary

of the Party in March 1985—and began to sound more like a member of the old internationalist wing of the Republican Party than like the New Right. William Safire, the conservative *New York Times* op-ed columnist, lambasted Reagan for wanting early negotiations and said that the president "had fairly got down on his knees" in his eagerness for a personal meeting with Gorbachev. Safire charged that Reagan's "hots to hold hands has led to a significant weakening of his position on Russian violations of past arms agreements: what used to be his pointed objections to the placement of battle-management radar and the encryption of missile telemetry that mocks the ABM treaty has, overnight, become mere 'language problems between our two countries.'"[3] In May 1985 the flourishing but still not entirely triumphant neocon establishment held a conference specifically designed to warn against any softening toward the Soviet Union and to remind everyone of the weakness of American intellectuals for socialism and communism.

One of the more unintentionally hilarious speeches at the conference, held in Washington's posh Madison hotel, was delivered by the novelist Tom Wolfe. As Sidney Blumenthal, who would later become an aide to Bill Clinton, recounts:

When the main course of polemics was cleared away
and only dessert remained, the writer Tom Wolfe was
served up. He wore pastels, the crowd wore gray.
None dared call it chic. The ideological spoilsmen—
conservative intellectuals with think-tank sinecures,
foundation executives, political operatives, and federal jobholders[—]were congratulated on their
"courage" for appearing at this lush affair in Reagan's
Washington, incidentally funded in part by the State
Department. Then came the rote attack on the New
Class, those who really have power, "a class of ruling
intellectuals trained to rule a country," Wolfe declared. The appeal of Marxism, he explained was due
to its "implicit secret promise . . . of handing power
over to intellectuals." . . . The conservatives applauded, dispersed into the Washington night, and
showed up at their New Class jobs the next morning.[4]

Given the widespread knowledge in 1985 of Stalin's
purges of intellectuals (including those who had strongly
supported the Bolsehviks), it is hard to imagine that any
significant American intellectual, at any point on the political spectrum, still believed in an "implicit secret promise" that eggheads would assume power in any Communist dictatorship.

The neocons were trying to prevent exactly what soon happened: a popular and conservative American president, reelected by an overwhelming margin, saw nothing to lose and everything to gain by negotiating with a man he saw as a new kind of Soviet leader. Only two and a half years later, in December 1987, a smiling, joking Gorbachev and an equally ebullient Reagan met in Washington to sign an agreement to eliminate medium- and short-range nuclear missiles. A national poll, conducted at the time of Gorbachev's visit to the United States, found that almost as many Americans had a favorable impression of Gorbachev (59 percent) as of Reagan (63 percent). And 85 percent thought that Gorbachev was more interested in improving relations with the United States than previous Soviet leaders.[5] Gorbachev's entire trip to Washington was a right-winger's nightmare, as everyone from congressional leaders to holiday tourists in the nation's capital struggled to make some sort of personal contact with "Gorby." On his final day in Washington, Gorbachev horrified both his KGB and Secret Service security details—the two agencies were cooperating to keep the Soviet leader safe—by getting out of his car and shaking hands of "thrilled passersby" at Connecticut Avenue and L Street; meeting at the Soviet embassy with a group of local high school students who had been trying for days to meet him; and declaring at a final press conference that he found the teenagers "remarkable" and that young people, unlike their elders, are able to "quickly find a common tongue."[6]

Conservatives had applauded earlier in 1987 when Reagan, on a visit to Germany, had issued his famous challenge: "Mr. Gorbachev, tear down this wall!" But the right wing was stunned when, in 1989, Germans themselves did tear down the wall and the Soviet government did nothing to stop them. Even then, as many Eastern European countries were moving out of the Soviet orbit and embracing democracy, conservative intellectuals like Podhoretz and conservative Kremlinologists like Zbigniew Brzezinski were still warning that it was only a matter of time until Gorbachev sent the Red Army in to restore the status quo, as Nikita Khrushchev had in Hungary in 1956 and Leonid Brezhnev had in Czechoslovakia in 1968. When Gorbachev did no such thing, and his policies led to the dissolution of the Soviet Union in 1991, the conservative hawks tripped over one another to take credit for "winning" the Cold War and promptly developed amnesia about their dissatisfaction with Reagan's willingness to negotiate during the mid-1980s. Gorbachev himself had been a gradualist; he hoped that it would be possible to remove fear from Soviet society and end censorship without destroying Communist authority altogether. In the end, all it took was a lessening of fear to accelerate the collapse of the old order. It is beyond the scope of this book to explore the complexity of the reasons—personal, social, and economic—for Gorbachev's political demise and the breakup of the Soviet Union or to differentiate between whatever role U.S. foreign policy played and the larger role of internal pressures in Soviet society. Regardless of the ending, Gorbachev's reformist course during the eighties should logically have improved the standing of an internationalist like Hiss, who had always believed in negotiation rather than confrontation. Such a man might, conceivably, have been seen by the American public in the eighties as someone who simply had the misfortune to have been ahead of his time. The question of whether or not Hiss had been a Communist might have come to seem much less important to a new generation of Americans, whose image of a Soviet leader was not Stalin, not the shoe-pounding Khrushchev, not the dull, geriatric mediocrity of Brezhnev but the sophisticated, educated, and reasonable Gorbachev.

There were several reasons why the friendlier, Gorbachev-inspired climate of American public opinion toward the Soviet Union did not produce any revival of support for Hiss. First, Hiss was considered a man of the past even by journalists who were still interested in his case. Remnick, for instance, either failed to ask Hiss what he thought of Gorbachev or considered the answer too uninteresting to include in his profile of Hiss. Many of Hiss's contemporaries, such as George Kennan, had a great deal to say about the changes in the Soviet Union during the Gorbachev era, but they were not, of course, constrained by having been Cold War icons—whether as victims or villains. Second, Hiss was still, in spite of the denial of his *coram nobis* petition, dedicated to somehow proving his innocence (as would become clear after the fall of the Soviet Union, when he would make a concerted effort to obtain vindication through new information released from KGB files). Because Hiss was so sharply focused on reversing the judgments of the past, he could not benefit from any contemporary changes in public attitudes toward the Soviets.

Finally, Hiss never really recovered from the damage that Weinstein's book did to his campaign for rehabilitation. The best he could do with younger journalists who viewed him with skepticism, but not without sympathy, was to portray himself as an ambiguous figure rather than as someone about whom all the important questions had been answered beyond a reasonable doubt. In the conclusion of his long piece in the *Washington Post*, Remnick predicted that the story of the Hiss case, when it was eventually retold in Hiss's obituary, "will end in ambiguity." Hiss's persistence in asserting his innocence, Remnick wrote, "gives him the *possibility* of martyrdom, even if he is probably not one. It has helped him win friends, loyal defenders. It has made him more important than he ever could have been, either as a loyal servant to Franklin Roosevelt or to the Communist Party. Ambiguity has been a savior to him."[7]

The Enemy Vanishes, 1992–2008

The very word *ambiguity* infuriates the political right when applied to Alger Hiss, because it suggests that there is still some doubt, however minuscule, about his guilt. When Mikhail Gorbachev was replaced by Boris Yeltsin and the Soviet Union came to an official end on December 31, 1991, Hiss's defenders and detractors both had reason to hope that access to long-classified espionage documents, in the Soviet Union as well as the United States, would write a conclusion not only to Hiss's case but to many other disputed episodes in the Cold War. Yeltsin himself promised to open previously closed archives to Russian and Western scholars with a special interest in Soviet history. Six months after the collapse of the Soviet Union, Hiss—who was then eighty-eight years old—made written requests to several Russian officials that he be allowed to search for evidence that he was "never a paid, contracted agent for the Soviet Union." This was a carefully constructed phrase. No one, including Chambers, had ever suggested that Hiss was paid for providing intelligence to the Soviet Union. On the contrary: if you believed, as congressional investigators did, that government agencies were honeycombed with American Communists willing to hand over classified information to the Soviets, the most horrifying aspect was that they did so out of idealism rather than as paid professionals. One former Soviet official, General Dmitri A. Volkogonov, met in Moscow with the historian and pro-Hiss scholar John Lowenthal—a representative chosen by Hiss—and agreed to search Soviet archives for information. Volkogonov, by then a military adviser to Yeltsin, had long been an official Soviet historian, overseeing, among other projects, the massive *History of the Great Patriotic War* (as Russians call the Second World War). A month after the initial meeting in Moscow, Volkogonov presented Lowenthal with a letter declaring that he had found "not a single document . . . that substantiates the allegation that Mr. A. Hiss collaborated with the intelligence sources of the Soviet Union." Therefore, Volkogonov said, Hiss "had never and nowhere been recruited as an agent of the intelligence services of the U.S.S.R." Volkogonov added, in videotaped remarks, that he had also looked for material about Whittaker Chambers and found that while Chambers had indeed been a member of the American Communist Party, there was no evidence that he had been a spy. (Hiss, of course, had long maintained that Chambers's espionage activities were as much a fantasy as his story about being a close friend of Hiss's in the Party.)

Although Hiss and his supporters claimed that Volkogonov's findings conclusively proved Hiss's innocence, there was immediate skepticism, and not only from those who had staked their careers on Hiss's guilt, about whether Volkogonov could possibly have thoroughly inspected all archives in the relatively short period between his first contact with Lowenthal and his public statement. The dedicated Hiss-haters on the right were indignant about the television coverage of Volkogonov's statement, but the truth is that the entire story was immediately swallowed up by the closing days of the 1992 presidential campaign. The *New York Times* buried the story on page 14 of the B section. In his third paragraph, *Times* reporter David Margolick introduced the skepticism of many scholars about Volkogonov's findings. "Scholars of Soviet affairs said they were struck by the categorical, almost passionate, nature of the Russian official's statement," Margolick wrote. "They said that as a respected historian and close adviser to President Boris Yeltsin, General Volkogonov should be taken seriously. But they cautioned that given the labyrinthine nature of the Soviet bureaucracy and the sensitivity of military and foreign intelligence operations, General Volkogonov may have unknowingly overstated his findings." Hiss was quoted in the same story as saying that he expected such reactions from his detractors, who would only accept evidence from Soviet archives if it proved to be incriminating. "They're so committed to their point of view that it's psychologically impossible for them to be open-minded," Hiss added.[1] In the *New Yorker*, Hiss's son, Tony, joyfully asserted that that Volkogonov's findings had exonerated his father and that everyone would now know "what my family and my father's devoted friends and well-wishers have always known—that Alger Hiss was not a Communist, not a spy, not a traitor." Tony wrote that his father's long travails had "suddenly been given a very happy public ending, and I'm still finding what has happened almost too good to be true."[2] It was too good to be true. Volkogonov soon began to hedge, and he then retracted his statement in an interview with Serge Schmemann, a

Moscow correspondent for the *Times*. He told Schmemann that he had looked through only KGB files and that
he had no access to military intelligence files. (Chambers
had worked for the GRU, the Soviet military intelligence
arm, not the KGB.) Volkogonov said that he had been "a
bit taken aback" by the suggestion that he had found conclusive evidence clearing Hiss. "Hiss wrote that he was 88
and would like to die peacefully, that he wanted to prove
that he was never a paid, contracted spy," Volkogonov explained. "What I said gives no basis to claim a full
clarification. There's no guarantee that it [Hiss's file] was
not destroyed, that it was not in other channels."[3] Moreover, Volkogonov acknowledged that he had spent only
two days searching the archives—hardly time enough to
unearth the entire records of paid or unpaid intelligence
agents over a period of a decade. When I read Schmemann's story in December 1992, I had to go back and look
for the original *Times* article, which I had missed because
it was hidden in the B section. If I had read only the later
accounts of the news coverage of this episode from anti-
Hiss historians, who constantly label the press pro-Hiss, I
would have mistakenly concluded that the first story had
been in the A-section and the retraction had been buried.
"Volkogonov's retraction did not gain anything like the
attention among American media that his initial memo-

randum had garnered," G. Edward White states flatly.[4] This assertion typifies the conspiratorial spin placed on any story about Hiss by both the true believers in his innocence and those who regard belief in Hiss's guilt as a litmus test not only of political loyalty but of scholarly seriousness and common sense. The *Nation* had described Volkogonov's findings as an "apparent vindication of Hiss after all these years" and said that it awaited with "glorious anticipation" the heartburn that "neoconservatives and far-right communities" were bound to experience as a result of the new evidence. The editorial did, however, issue an important caveat about "the hazards of relying on K.G.B. and other intelligence agency documents or the lack of them."[5] That indeed has proved to be the crux of the factual, as distinct from ideological, disputes over new documents emerging from both Soviet and American intelligence files since the six-week wonder of the Volkogonov story. In addition to realizing that he had spoken too soon on the basis of too little evidence, Volkogonov might also have been told by more prudent Russian government officials that Russia itself had little to gain from involving itself in a bitter American historical controversy.

In the early years after the disintegration of the Soviet Union, both American and Russian scholars were allowed tantalizing glimpses into formerly closed files of Soviet and American intelligence agencies. The most important of these were documents from the Comintern (the international organization that supervised Communist Parties outside the Soviet Union) and from the American Communist Party. These were housed in a Russian archive called the Russian Center for the Preservation and Study of Documents of Recent History (the Russian acronym, RTsKhIDNI, sounds like *ritzkidney* when native English-speakers pronounce it). The second important set of documents, known as the Venona files, came from the U.S. National Security Agency. These files include intercepted cables from Soviet intelligence agents to Moscow from, roughly, 1942 to 1946—a period when the Soviets were unaware that American intelligence agencies had broken their code. Scholarly analyses of both sets of files were published by the Yale University Press. The first, *The Secret World of American Communism*, by Harvey Klehr, John Earl Haynes, and Fridrikh Igorevich Firsov, appeared in 1995. The second volume (and they ought to be read as companions), *Venona*, by Haynes and Klehr, was published in 1999. The *ritzkidney* files do not contain a single document that directly mentions Hiss; what they do provide is considerable evidence backing up Chambers's and Elizabeth Bentley's testimony about the organized spying of *some* American Communists. The Venona files do contain decoded communications that mention a Soviet agent by the name of "Ales," and Haynes and Klehr conclude that "it is difficult to imagine its [the Ales reference] fitting anyone but Hiss." If Hanes and Klehr are right, Hiss was still a Soviet agent at the time of the Yalta conference. A decoded Venona cable dated March 5, 1945, states, "After the Yalta Conference, when he had gone on to Moscow, a Soviet personage in a very responsible position [Ales gave to understand that it was Comrade Vishinski]* allegedly got in touch with Ales and at the behest of the Military Neighbors (the GRU) passed on to him their gratitude and so on." On the basis of this cable, Klehr and Haynes argue:

> This passage indicates that Ales had been at the Yalta conference and had returned to the United States through Moscow. After the . . . conference, most of the American delegation returned directly to the United States from Iran. Those Americans attending from the U.S. embassy in Moscow returned to Moscow but did not, as Ales did, then proceed quickly to the United States. . . . There was, however, a small party of four State Depart-

---

*Andrei Vishinski was the notorious Soviet prosecutor in the purge trials of 1937–1938. He served as Stalin's foreign minister from 1949 to 1953 and, after Stalin's death, became the permanent Soviet delegate to the United Nations.

ment officials who flew to Moscow to wrap up some
details with the Soviets and then proceeded after a
brief layover to Washington. There has never been
any allegation or evidence that three of them—Secretary of State Edward Stettinius, Director of the
Office of European Affairs H. Freeman Matthews,
and Wilder Foote, Stettinius's press aide—were
Soviet agents. The fourth official was Alger Hiss.[6]

The inference that Haynes and Klehr draw from the
Venona communication about "Ales" has frequently been
described as a smoking gun, but I find it difficult to place
total faith in the information that one intelligence agent
passes on to another. Spies are by definition in the business of lying, and I find it easy enough to believe that a
Soviet agent in the United States (or an American agent
in the Soviet Union) might imply that he had high-level
assets who did not really exist—and that he knew more
about their activities and movements than he really did.
(Reading espionage cables tends to turn anyone into either a conspiracy theorist or an anti–conspiracy theorist
—sometimes both. I wonder why an agent whose real
name is Alger would choose or be assigned a code name as
similar-sounding as Ales.) Nevertheless, the Venona files
certainly supply a loaded—whether smoking or not—

gun to those who believe that Hiss was guilty as charged and that the attempt by his supporters to portray him as an innocent victim of the Cold War only proves that certain liberal intellectuals are and always have been on the wrong side of history. I actually thought, at the turn of the millennium, that the Soviet intelligence documents released during the Yeltsin years would prove to be the last possible twist in the Hiss case—that both sides would have to be content with chewing over old information. But no. At a conference sponsored in 2007 by the Nation Institute, Kai Bird and Svetlana Chervonnaya, a historian and archival researcher based in Moscow, concluded that the "Ales" cable referred not to Hiss but to his State Department colleague Wilder Foote. Bird and Chervonnaya (an extremely well regarded researcher in Moscow), who documented their research in a lengthy paper published in the *American Scholar* in 2007, offered elaborate findings suggesting that Hiss's travels immediately after Yalta did not fit the criteria for "Ales," but Foote's did. The problem with this argument, as with absolute reliance on the Venona files, is that to consider it credible, you must accept the assumption that the movements of spies and their handlers are accurately reflected in documents compiled by spies and their handlers. Furthermore, the naming of Foote (who is not alive to defend himself), based on highly speculative interpretations of secret communications, recalled the hearsay evidence and guilt by association that defined so many McCarthyite accusations—and that have justly elicited condemnation from civil libertarians for the past half-century. By the nineties, when the first intelligence documents were declassified after the collapse of the Soviet Union, any scholar who sought access to Cold War espionage files could not possibly have been "neutral" on the subject of Hiss's guilt, and journalists have been even quicker than scholars to interpret the documents "aggressively"—an adverbial euphemism for filling in the blanks with one's own political biases. The Bird-Chervonnaya presentation received only a modest amount of publicity, but it provided the stimulus for a six-thousand-word blast in the *New Republic* by Sam Tanenhaus. The headline over Tanenhaus's article, "The End of the Journey," was an allusion to Lionel Trilling's novel, *The Middle of the Journey* (1947), which features a character based on Chambers. Tanenhaus, not surprisingly, has no more use for Bird and Chervonnaya's findings than he has for Alger Hiss, whom he describes as "a social and political type commonly found within its favored class in mature democracies: the covert enemy of an establishment who constantly trades on establishment privileges— snobbery, social pride, 'old school' ties, inveterate name-dropping."[7] There is something odd about this particular criticism of Hiss, given that snobbery, trading on old school ties, and inveterate name-dropping have always seemed to me characteristic traits of unabashed defenders as well as covert enemies of entrenched establishments. Indeed, any prevailing establishment is defined by its old-boy and -girl networks and the opportunity provided by those networks for dropping names (as distinct from naming names). Tanenhaus's screed, informed by the obsessiveness that characterizes almost every scholar of the Hiss case, elicited an equally impassioned counterblast from Jeff Kisseloff, editor of the pro-Hiss Web site sponsored by the Nation Institute at New York University. "The fictions, slurs, distortions, and inaccuracies about Hiss, some of them simply sloppy," Kisseloff writes, "are presented in a casually omniscient, reassuring voice. These misrepresentations often come attached to phrases such as 'it is well known that' or 'as everyone knows' or as 'we now know with certainty that.'"[8] Kisseloff might have pointed out, if he wanted to dabble in guilt by association, that "it is well known"—frequently coupled with "life itself teaches us" or "it is not by accident" (Stalin's favorite)—was also a phrase commonly used by every generation of Soviet propagandists. Despite the fact that the battle over the Hiss case is now more than sixty years old, the pro-

Hiss and anti-Hiss intellectuals seem to hate each other as much as their predecessors did when Joseph Stalin presided in the Kremlin and Joseph McCarthy was waving around his list of covert Communists in the State Department. Many no doubt hate one another personally, but what each side truly hates is the other's version of history.

Attitudes toward government itself—the activist government embodied by the New Deal—have played just as important a role as attitudes toward communism in the struggle over history that has polarized intellectual politics since the Reagan administration. The lasting resonance of the Hiss case is due, in no small measure, to his and Whittaker Chambers's involvement in the dispute over the domestic as well as the international legacies of the Roosevelt era. One reason why the anticommunist fever of the late forties and early fifties burned out so quickly was that the prosecutorial hunt for domestic communists could not be disentangled from right-wing hatred of the New Deal. But centrist Republicans, beginning with Dwight Eisenhower, largely accepted the domestic legacy of the Roosevelt years, including Social Security, federal aid to education, and the GI Bill. They understood that the public was not about to embrace an anticommunism based on the premise that a large proportion of leaders in Roosevelt's administration had been disloyal to their country. People like my parents may have seen Hiss as a traitor, but they were not about to swallow the right-wing thesis that the New Deal was dominated by communist sympathizers attempting to further communist goals. Liberal anti-Communist historians, most notably Arthur Schlesinger, Jr., made an effective case for a U.S. government policy based on the principle that while Soviet Communism was a threat to America, communism was not a significant threat *in* America. The New Deal itself was seen, except from the far right, not as an ideologically driven attempt to shift the balance of power from unrestrained business to government but as a pragmatic effort to correct some of the worst evils of unrestrained capitalism, such as the lack of regulation that had caused millions to lose their life savings in the stock market and failed banks. The last major government program with origins in the reformist spirit of the thirties was Medicare, and the widespread public enthusiasm for what the right-wingers darkly portrayed as the first step toward "socialized medicine" only confirmed what centrist historians and politicians had long believed about the pragmatism of the New Deal—and about the public's approval of government safety nets that protected the middle class as well as the poor. During the Reagan years, however, the idea that the New Deal had really been a centralized plan to restructure the American economy along anticapitalist lines (or, at the very least, a carefully thought-out, coordinated plan to shift the balance of power from business to government) began to make a comeback. In spite of his economic conservatism, Reagan—unlike his ideological descendant George W. Bush—was too adept a politician to frighten the public by insisting on big changes in programs like Medicare and Social Security. But a younger generation of right-wing ideologists, whose ideas were not disseminated to mass audiences until Bush's campaign in 2000, was already intent on the long-term goal of reversing many of the assumptions and programs originating in the New Deal. The shift to the right was evident not only in the eighties but during the Clinton years, when financial markets were deregulated to a degree that would have been unthinkable in other post–New Deal Democratic administrations. The mainstreaming of once-conservative ideas produced a new generation of "neoliberal" politicians and intellectuals who did not share the assumptions of Schlesinger's generation about the ways in which government might be used as a force for good.

Tanenhaus's 1997 biography of Chambers, deservedly praised for its demonstration that Chambers was a much more complex and interesting character than his portrayal in the demonology of anti-anticommunism, was also strongly influenced by neoliberal revisionist views of the New Deal. While criticizing Chambers's autobiography for its ideological rigidity, Tanenhaus also asserts that there is "a spark of intuitive insight" in the commentary on domestic politics in *Witness*. "I saw that the New Deal was only superficially a reform movement," Chambers declared in one of these moments of so-called insight. Instead, Chambers argued, "the New Deal was a genuine revolution, whose deepest purpose was not simply reform within existing traditions, but a basic change in the social, and, above all, the power relationships within the nation. It was not a revolution by violence. It was a revolution by bookkeeping and lawmaking."[9] Tanenhaus notes that Chambers's analysis of the New Deal drew a good deal of criticism in contemporary reviews of his book, but argues that "there is more truth in [it] than Chambers's critics could see in 1952." At that time, most scholars agreed with "consensus historians" like Schlesinger and Richard Hofstadter, who viewed the New Deal more as a series of brilliant improvisations than as a planned, consistent program for social and governmental change. As Tanenhaus notes, a number of younger scholars during the past two decades have portrayed the New Deal as a more centralized, ideologically driven plan than the previous generation of eminent historians did. In the revisionist take, FDR's administration is seen more as an attempt to establish a new system of "state capitalism" than as an ad hoc series of reforms.[10] But are the revisionists right in their portrayal of a more centralized New Deal, or are they taking a contrarian position vis-à-vis their elders because the center of American politics has shifted to the right since 1980? If historiographical fashion is any guide, another generation will come along and meld the recent revisionist scholarship about the New Deal with the older historians' analysis, thereby offering something for everyone and something to offend everyone. But there is no question that in the hands of the political right today, the view of the New Deal as a centralized, intentional plan to remake American society lends itself to the contention that many New Dealers were really socialists or communists who wanted to remake the U.S. economy in an "un-American" mold. This argument has played a significant role in keeping the Hiss fires burning, because one of Hiss's defenses was always that he had been attacked precisely because he was a loyal New Dealer—not because anyone really thought he was a Communist Party member. For those on the far right, Hiss's history as a New Dealer always strengthened rather than weakened the indictment against him as a Communist, and some right-wing bottom-feeders have no compunction about distorting legitimate revisionist New Deal scholarship to revive the charge that the Roosevelt administration was honeycombed with dedicated Stalinists working to turn the United States into a Bolshevik dictatorship. For liberals today (including those who consider Hiss guilty as well as the minority who still believe that he might have been framed) the right-wing linkage between Hiss and a "pinko" New Deal is particularly inflammatory. The Bush administration never concealed its desire to privatize government programs that have provided a security net since the Roosevelt years, and liberal frustration at having to fight an unending battle on behalf of FDR's liberal domestic legacy has fused, to a considerable extent, with battles over foreign policy and intelligence gathering. Political change and the passage of time may defuse the argument over the inheritance of the New Deal (although the fierce, continuing debate about the legacy of the Enlightenment suggests otherwise), but the profound intellectual and political division over the relationship between anticommunism and patriotism shows no signs of abating. The identity of the enemy has changed, but the issues raised by the Hiss case about dissent, loyalty, and patriotism have not.

Passions as Epilogue

> The problem now, for a nation built on a few ideas
> about liberty shared with triumphant innocence by one
> generation in the 1780s, was how to protect the in-
> nocent citizen from getting pinched between the reality
> of the threat and the epidemic fear of it.
> —ALISTAIR COOKE, *A Generation on Trial*, 1950

On the Fourth of July weekend in 2000, the *New York
Times* published a conversation about patriotism between
Norman Podhoretz, the longtime neoconservative war-
rior and editor of *Commentary*, and Victor Navasky, who,
as publisher of the *Nation*, was as strongly identified with
the political and cultural left as Podhoretz was with the
right. In one exchange, the moderator quoted Samuel
Johnson's remark that patriotism "is the last refuge of a
scoundrel" and asked both men whether patriotism had
"gone out of style" in the United States. Podhoretz, as
befitted the author of a forthcoming book titled *My Love
Affair with America*, replied:

Well, I think that Johnson was wrong and this was a
most uncharacteristic remark for him, a fervent
Tory, to have made, since conservatives, generally
in Europe anyway, had been associated with patriotic sentiment and nationalist sentiment. Has patriotism gone out of style in America? The answer is
certainly yes, as of very recently. But my own feeling is that it's slowly coming back. We see signs
of this resurgence of patriotic sentiment in various
sectors of the culture. The most salient, I suppose,
would be the enormous success of Tom Brokaw's
two books on the World War II generation. I think
the success of a movie like *Saving Private Ryan* is
another sign, a sign of new respect for the kind of
virtues that were traditionally associated with patriotism or love of country.

Navasky, the author of *Naming Names* (1984), a history of
the impact of the postwar anticommunist crusade on the
entertainment community, retorted:

Well, about Samuel Johnson, Ambrose Bierce had
an amendment to Johnson. I think he said, "I beg to
submit, sir, it is the first." In other words, patriotism is not the last refuge of scoundrels, it's the first.
I don't agree with that. I would suggest that in the

Vietnam era the people who were protesting the war included a large number of patriots. My definition of patriotism would involve fighting to make sure that your country lives up to its highest ideals. And from that perspective even those who burn the flag—not all of them but some of them—may have been as patriotic as those who wrapped themselves in the flag. So the word may be coming back in some way, but the struggles to make America the best it can be have been going on, it seems to me, since the Revolutionary War.[1]

Podhoretz replied sharply that "struggling to make the country live up to its best ideals has in practice generally meant denigrating the country for not doing so." Navasky countered with the argument that from the abolitionist movement to the civil rights movement, "those people who fought to achieve the American dream of equal rights for all" were initially described and dismissed as unpatriotic and then, in the twentieth century, as Communists. This discussion took place more than fourteen months before the terrorist attacks of September 11, 2001, when patriotism, melded with fear, outrage, and an unmistakable component of vengeance, would make a comeback to a degree that had not been observable since the height of the Cold War. The new enemy, radical Islamism, now occupies some of the political, psychological, and emotional space that communism occupied for politically aware Americans—especially intellectuals—in the late forties and early fifties. For those whose political consciousness was shaped for decades by their antipathy toward Soviet Communism and the hunt for American Communists, the new world of Islamist terrorism, and its threat to the United States and Western democratic values, provides another organizing principle for thinking about America and the world. This generalization applies less strongly to centrist liberals (the group from which anti-Communist liberals had been drawn) and to moderate conservatives than it does to the those at the farthest right and left wings of political discourse. It is the political right, however, that has explicitly connected those who considered the hunt for domestic Communists a much greater threat to America than communism itself with those who oppose the war in Iraq and the Bush administration's abridgement of civil liberties in service to the war on terror. In 2003, as new revelations about the Bush administration's domestic spying under the Patriot Act were coming to light, Ann Coulter, the Bad Blonde Witch of the Right, was flogging her book *Treason: Liberal Treachery from the Cold War to the War on Terror.* Appearing on the *Today* show, Coulter confided that she was thrilled by the liberal objections to the Bush's administration's wiretapping without a court order, because the complaints of civil libertarians were demonstrating once again that "liberals can't be trusted with the security of our nation—from Stalin to Saddam." There it is: *From Stalin to Saddam*. These are words to live by for the hard right, of whatever generation, just as they are words to ignite unapologetic political enmity in liberals of every generation. In this heated climate, it is not surprising that the Hiss case continues to surface as a marker of loyalty. As Jacob Weisberg, editor of the online magazine *Slate*, observes, "the deeper you delve into such battles, the greater the feeling grows that these are not primarily arguments about historical fact at all. Espionage charges, initiated by subterranean and frequently unreliable sources, are a way of arguing about the past as if it were still present, a continuing of ideological politics by other means. . . . Listening in, you get the sense that these arguments are less a posthumous sorting out of the cold war than a sublimated continuation of it."[2] Weisberg was writing in 1999, before Cold War premises and language were transferred, in both the literal and psychoanalytic senses, to debates about the war on terror. He was responding to yet another round of analysis of Soviet intelligence files (*The*

Haunted Wood, by the bloodhound Allen Weinstein and
Alexander Vassiliev, a former KGB officer and historian),
which persuaded a number of holdout historians of the
left—and on the left—to throw in the towel on Hiss.
"Let's face it, the debate just ended," said Maurice Isserman, professor of history at Hamilton College.[3] Isserman
is considered one of the best scholars in the young generation of historians who, beginning in the late 1970s and
1980s, challenged the view that the Soviet Union was entirely responsible for the Cold War and argued against
monolithic portrayals of the American left as overly sympathetic to communism. In his interview with Weisberg,
he was reflecting the views of a fair number of middle-
aged intellectuals who came of age during the sixties, had
not been convinced of Hiss's guilt in the seventies and
eighties, but changed their minds as new information
from Soviet and American files became available in the
nineties. (The way in which Weinstein and Vassiliev
gained access to the documents cited in *The Haunted Wood*
forms yet another ironic chapter in the history of the end
of the Cold War. Their publisher, Random House, paid a
considerable sum of money—by some accounts, more
than a million dollars—to a Russian organization called
the Association of Retired Intelligence Officers. Thus, in
return for their authors' being allowed to catch a glimpse

of previously unexamined Stalin-era KGB files, Random House forked over a pension for former KGB officials—a stellar example of the "market economy" in action in both countries.)

If there is a consensus about Hiss's personal guilt among most liberals as well as among conservatives, there is no consensus about whether American interests were damaged more by the activities of American Communists or by the anticommunist campaign that also ensnared many leftists who never imagined that people they knew were conspiring in cafeterias and purloining government documents. This is exactly where the past meets the present, because the same debate is now being conducted over torture, the rights of detainees at Guantánamo, and government wiretapping of American citizens. Are we doing more damage to ourselves than terrorists could ever do when the U.S. government engages in practices that liberals consider "un-American" in a sense diametrically opposed to the McCarthy-era usage of the term? Are we engaging in "denigrating the country," as Podhoretz puts it, if we insist that parsing the meaning of torture disgraces the ideals upon which our nation was founded? Or are those who refuse to condemn such government actions implicitly denigrating the country by holding it to a lower standard of decency? How do we identify the tipping point at which an external threat is so overwhelming that it outweighs any concern about the protection of the rights of those who might pose an internal threat? The last question lay at the heart of the debate over the legislative hunt for American Communists after the Second World War, and although the enemy has changed, the divergent views about the essence of patriotism, expressed forcefully by Podhoretz and Navasky, have not.

In this continuing debate, attitudes toward the social convulsions of the sixties, and toward the New Left, figure as prominently as attitudes toward the Old Left of the thirties. The older generation of neoconservatives, like Podhoretz, saw the protests of the sixties as unpatriotic and anti-American. *Commentary* magazine, under Podhoretz's editorship in the early seventies, may have started the trend of referring to "the Movement" of the sixties as if it had been a disciplined organization like the American Communist Party of the thirties. Many on the left, from the civil rights struggle through the women's drive for equal rights, also referred to themselves as members of movements, but there was no centralized discipline or monolithic point of view implied by the term. In his 1979 memoir *Breaking Ranks*, Podhoretz lumps together former Attorney General Ramsey Clark, the op-ed page of the *New York Times*, and the American Civil

Liberties Union as fellow travelers. "On questions ranging from crime to the nature of art, from drugs to economic growth, from ecology to the new egalitarianism,"
Podhoretz asserts, "the dogmas of the Movement—both
in their unexpurgated state and in the sanitized versions
that had by now become the conventional wisdom of the
fellow-traveling culture laying claim to the epithet [*sic*]
'liberal'—*Commentary* became the perhaps the single
most visible scourge of the Movement within the intellectual community."[4] The next generation of conservatives, however, was also coming of age in the sixties. A few
were actually participants in the demonic "Movement"
and eventually underwent a conversion to conservatism
reminiscent of the thirties' Communists who discovered
that their God had failed them. It was much easier for the
refugees from the New Left to condemn their past precisely because, unlike the Communist Party members of
the thirties, the protesters of the sixties were never subject to the internal and external controls that had applied
to Party members. More commonly, though, conservatives who came of age in the sixties were disgusted right
from the start by the rebellion of their contemporaries on
the left—although most of the future hawks, protected
by student draft deferments, were no more eager than
their left-wing counterparts to serve in Vietnam. An ex-

traordinary number of the prominent right-wingers who were young in the sixties, helped create the "Reagan revolution" in the eighties, and promoted the war in Iraq under Bush, have direct ties, by blood or marriage, to the founding generation of neoconservatives whose views were shaped either during the 1930s or in the decade after the Second World War. Elliott Abrams is the son-in-law of Norman Podhoretz and Midge Decter. Bill Kristol, editor and founder of the *Weekly Standard,* one of the staunchest supporters of the Iraq war, and now a conservative op-ed columnist for the *New York Times,* is Irving Kristol's and Gertrude Himmelfarb's son. John Podhoretz, who has inherited the editorship of *Commentary* (in an intellectual if not a legal sense), is of course Norman's son. Podhoretz the Younger, who gets testy when the issue of nepotism is raised, is as outspoken in his contempt for liberals—and in his view of liberals as unpatriotic—as his father. Asked in an interview whether he reads such opposition publications as the *Nation* or the *New York Review of Books,* he responded that the *New York Review* is "what it's been for 35 or 40 years, which is a highly sophisticated vehicle for anti-American self-hatred."[5] Podhoretz fils also dismissed journalistic critics like Eric Alterman, who had described his appointment as an act of cronyism rather than meritocracy. The editor-

designate of *Commentary* said that Alterman was motivated by resentment at Podhoretz for having refused to
shake his hand twenty years ago. "Why is that?" asked the
interviewer. "Shouldn't you make some pretense of civility toward your fellow writers?" Podhoretz answered that
"making a pretense of civility toward Eric Alterman is
like making a pretense of civility to a scorpion." Alterman, as it happens, has written extensively and critically
about press coverage of revelations concerning the Hiss
case during the past fifteen years. Public statements like
Podhoretz's comparison of Alterman to a scorpion (imagine what such people say about one another privately!)
elicit a certain sense of relief that most of the intellectuals
involved in this battle over history live in New York and
Washington, two cities whose gun possession laws are
among the strictest in the nation.

The targeted and unabashed contempt that many
right-wing and left-wing intellectuals have for each other
has helped to propel the Hiss controversy into the
twenty-first century. Right-wing intellectuals tend to
avoid the intellectual label, because they have been extremely successful at turning the very word *intellectual*
into a pejorative synonym for liberal. The neoconservative patriarch Irving Kristol, in *Reflections of a Neoconser-*

vative (1983), observed that although "intellectuals" were alienated from "the American way of life," the American people were not. "It is the self-imposed assignment of neoconservatism to explain to the American people why they are right," Kristol explained, "and to the intellectuals why they are wrong."[6] The right-wing linkage of intellectualism with "anti-American" liberalism—and with an overweening desire for power—has now made its way into the writings of authors not generally associated with the political right. Consider what Sam Tanenhaus—and any editor of the *Times Book Review* must, by his job definition, be pretty much of a centrist—had to say about left-wing intellectuals as a class in his *New Republic* article attacking the research of Kai Bird. Tanenhaus quoted George Orwell, who wrote in 1946 that English intellectuals began to display an interest in Soviet Russia only after the regime had become unmistakably totalitarian. That interest, Orwell, said, was rooted in the intellectuals' "wish to destroy the old, equalitarian version of Socialism and usher in a hierarchical society where the intellectual can at last get his hands on the whip."[7] Tanenhaus asserted that Orwell's observation "is no less true today" because "the intellectual left, most conspicuously in its Ivy League, Manhattan, and Hollywood variants, still clings to its dream of the whip handle, just as the educated right dreams of the day when the intelligentsia will be the first to feel the stinging cord."[8]

There they go again. Tanenhaus uses the word *intelligentsia* in precisely the same fashion as Ronald Reagan used it in his 1984 speech at Eureka College—to denigrate left-wing American intellectuals. Note that Tanenhaus speaks only of an "educated" right and avoids describing right-wingers either as intellectuals or as an intelligentsia. This notion of cabals of left-wing intellectuals dreaming about wielding whips instead of words is a comical anachronism, although there certainly are right-wing intellectuals in Washington who have not only been dreaming about but actually making policy to initiate military actions. (I don't think that any members of the liberal intelligentsia were among those defending the actions of military officers and defense department officials who initially turned a blind eye to the literal whip-wielding that took place at Abu Ghraib.) In the same 1946 essay, Orwell made another observation (which Tanenhaus does not quote) that goes a long way toward explaining the durability of Cold War controversies at a time when radical Islam appears to be the chief enemy of the West. Orwell wrote about the tendency "to foresee only *a continuation of the thing that is happening*. Now the tendency to do this is not only a bad habit, like inaccuracy or exaggeration. . . . It is a major mental disease."[9] A natural companion disease is the tendency to see the past as an infallible guide to the present and the future—even if not only the actors but the underlying social conditions have undergone vast changes. Such distorted thinking has a good deal to do with the unwillingness of both the right and the left to let go of the Cold War—and with the aggrieved accusations of stupidity and downright malevolence that have repeatedly surfaced in scholarly, a.k.a. political, arguments over the Hiss case.

To view the Hiss case as a purely political drama, however, would be to deny the crucial and individual significance of Hiss's personality. Although the battle over the case is, at its core, a debate about the meaning of American history at what may well turn out to have been the apex of American power, there is no question that Hiss's opaque personality is a major element of what his defenders still call a "mystery" and what those convinced of his guilt call simple treachery. "Why would Hiss have lied for the rest of his life, after he had served his time, if he really had been Communist and a spy?" is the question posed, in one form or another, by those who continue to believe that even if Hiss did perjure himself about knowing Chambers, his stance was understandable within the context of Cold War hysteria. These defenders go on to argue that even if Hiss did transmit some confidential documents to Communists or Soviet sympathizers, that too was understandable—both before the Nazi-Soviet pact and after the United States and the Soviet Union became allies in the war. The argument goes something like this: *Why shouldn't our ally have had access to full information about our military intentions? And in the thirties, Stalin's government was opposing Hitler. Why shouldn't it have been helpful to us — not only to the Soviet Union — for the Soviets to have a better read on American intentions in Europe?* For Hiss to admit that he was lying all along, however, would have meant the loss of his iconic status as a man who was victimized simply because he was "the right size"—neither too prominent nor too insignificant—for a symbolic anti-communist prosecution and persecution.[10] An admission of having been a Communist or of having been a spy would also have been an admission that Hiss had deceived his family and closest friends for nearly a half-century. I cannot imagine anyone less likely than Hiss to come clean and make the case that having been a Party member was understandable within the context of the times in which he was considered one of the best and the brightest. From the day he left prison, Hiss's entire public and private identities depended on his insistence that he had been an innocent victim of anticommunist passions that led too many Americans to disregard the legal protections and governmental traditions that truly did differentiate the United States from both communist and fascist regimes. It is difficult to understand why anyone on the left thought that Hiss's adamant, lifelong assertion of his innocence proved that he really was innocent, and it is equally difficult to understand why anyone on the right thinks that Hiss's refusal to change his story is the best evidence that he was a committed Communist (perhaps even beyond the grave of Soviet Communism) and a master spy. Once a man tells the kind of lie that Hiss told, even if he was no longer a Communist at the time he told the first lie, how can he ever change his story? It has been suggested by many writers, perhaps under the pernicious influence of the popular notions of "repressed memory" that permeated the culture in the 1980s, that Hiss actually came to believe his own story. This strikes me as utterly fantastic, in the dictionary sense of "appearing as if conceived by an unrestrained imagination." Nothing in Hiss's writings or public actions (recall his carefully framed request for information from Soviet files that he was not a *paid* agent) suggested that he was ever anything but a man in full possession of his faculties, living a consciously designed double life.

I doubt that any further revelations, as diligent scholars continue to squeeze out and tease out more information from Cold War intelligence files, will put an end to the Hiss case for those who view the controversy not only as an issue of fact but as a metaphor for the fundamental dispute about the essence of patriotism that has created a wall of separation between many conservatives and many liberals. The divisions among intellectuals have also proliferated during the past twenty years as a result of the emergence of the neoliberals, many now in their forties and fifties, who—unlike the anti-Stalinist liberals of Schlesinger's generation—have accepted many of the old conservative premises about communism having been a menace from within the United States as well as from without. Today's neoliberals are animated by a fierce desire not to be caught on the wrong side of history by seeming insufficiently supportive of efforts to identify and neutralize threats to national security in the current era of global terrorism. Weisberg's suggestion that battles over Cold War espionage are "not primarily arguments about historical fact at all" but "a way of arguing about the past as if it were still present" gives only a hint of the ideological passion that animates those who remain preoccupied with the twentieth-century history of American-Soviet relations. There is a good deal of talk today, on both the left and the right, about the "lessons of the Cold War," but there is no agreement about what those lessons are. One lesson that clearly has not been learned, in view of American intelligence failures in the Middle East during the past fifteen years, is the necessity for rigorous skepticism about the findings of our own espionage establishment. There is a strong case to be made that internal treachery was, and is, less of a threat to American intelligence-gathering capabilities than sheer stupidity, combined with the tendency of bureaucrats to tell those in power what they want to hear. The unexpected collapse of the Soviet Union should certainly have underlined the truth of Orwell's observation about the dangers inherent in the general human tendency, shared by high government officials who bear the responsibility for grave decisions, to anticipate only a continuation of what is already happening. For years, arguably for decades, American intelligence agencies greatly underestimated the internal weaknesses of the Soviet system. This evaluation was frequently reported as fact in the American press, which often transmitted an exaggerated picture of Soviet capabilities, particularly in areas like science and education, to the American public. When my husband returned from Moscow at the end of 1971, after two years as the bureau chief of the *Washington Post,* he found it almost impossible to convince many of his journalistic colleagues (including the editors of the *Post*) that Soviet science, apart from areas vital to the military, was in a shambles as a result of decades of incompetent political interference with research. The memory of Sputnik, which generated such intense American fear of losing the space race—and all that might imply for the balance of power on earth—influenced an entire generation of journalists and, through them, public opinion. This is not to say that American policies, which forced the Soviets to maintain a bloated military establishment that they could not afford, did nothing to hasten the demise of a dysfunctional economic system that had long relied on its public's stoic acceptance of living standards that, except for the upper class in the Soviet Union's largest cities, resembled those of a third-world country. Reasonable people may certainly disagree about the relative importance of external and internal pressures in hastening the disintegration of the Soviet Union. But whatever the degree of importance assigned to American power, it is difficult to make a solid case that the hunt for subversives within the United States had any significant long-term effect on the outcome of the Cold War. In any event, the question of exactly what we won by outlasting the Soviet Union is sure to be raised anew as a result of Vladimir Putin's revival of Russian nationalism, fueled this time not by communist ideology but by superior oil reserves.

Why, then, does the Alger Hiss case still matter in such vastly changed geopolitical circumstances? Given that his guilt will never be proved to the satisfaction of his last remaining defenders, and that his innocence has never been considered a serious possibility by most intellectuals for the past quarter of a century, the real significance of his fate revolves around the question of whether the normal, self-correcting, legally sanctioned mechanisms of a democratic society can be trusted, in times of fear and genuine danger, to preserve national security without violating individual rights and constitutional traditions. I would argue that the Hiss case, including the historical aftermath as well as the original prosecution, offers a powerful argument in favor of maximum, not minimum, civil libertarian safeguards in times of real as well as perceived danger. Without the guilt by association tactics pioneered by HUAC and extended by McCarthy's Senate investigations, many on the left might have been more open to the possibility, at an earlier period of history, that Hiss really was guilty and that, whatever the motive, it is a bad idea to have people in sensitive government jobs passing on confidential information to any foreign government. The suggestion of some on the left that even if Hiss was a spy, there wasn't really anything so bad about that because the Soviet Union was our ally during the war cannot be reconciled with the left's support for the 1986 sentencing of Jonathan Pollard, who spied for the Israelis while working as an analyst in the U.S. Navy Department. As for the right—which always thought that Hiss got off too easily—history has rendered a verdict far more convincing than the decision by the jury in 1950. The historical guilty verdict, whether one agrees with it or not, has been reached through decades of debate, scholarship, and free inquiry. Scholarly criticism of the fast-and-loose slanders conflating Communists, fellow travelers, and liberals during the postwar anticommunist crusades has made every bit as important a contribution to the historical debate—about Hiss in particular and American Communism in general—as the perusal of Cold War espionage documents has.

The problem identified in 1950 by Alistair Cooke—of protecting innocent citizens from being caught between real threats and the fear of threats—is as urgent today as it was then. What truly denigrates the country is the argument that fear and danger are legitimate excuses for riding roughshod over the Bill of Rights in pursuit of the chimera of a security based on contempt for liberty. One of the saddest aspects of the Hiss case is that the man was unworthy of the belief he inspired in so many honorable Americans. The other sorrowful coda is that the misplaced faith inspired by Hiss is still being used to impugn the patriotism of those who believe that it is more, not less, important for this nation to live up to its highest ideals and legal traditions in times of danger than in times of complacent security.

Chronology

1904   Alger Hiss is born in Baltimore.

1907   Hiss's father commits suicide.

1926   Hiss graduates from Johns Hopkins University and enters Harvard Law School, where he becomes a protégé of future Supreme Court Justice Felix Frankfurter.

1929   Hiss graduates from Harvard Law and is selected for the prestigious post of secretary to Supreme Court Justice Oliver Wendell Holmes. In December he marries Priscilla Fansler Hobson and becomes stepfather to Timothy Hobson, her son by her first marriage.

1932   The Hisses move to New York City, where Alger joins the law firm Cotton, Franklin, Wright and Gordon, and he and Priscilla both become involved in left-wing political circles.

1933   Franklin D. Roosevelt is inaugurated as president of the United States, and Hiss leaves for Washington to join the New Deal brain trust as an aide in the Agricultural Adjustment Administration.

1934   Hiss becomes counsel to a Senate subcommittee investigating profiteering by the munitions industry during World War I.

Near the end of the year, Hiss meets a freelance writer he will later say he knew only as "George Crosley." Crosley's real name is Whittaker Chambers, who will, fourteen years later, testify before Congress that he and Hiss were members of an underground Communist group, and that Hiss knew him not only under his own name but under his agent's name of Carl. Hiss will deny the charge until his death.

1935   Hiss and Crosley become better acquainted. Hiss rents Crosley an apartment, allows him and his family to spend several nights in a guest room in his home, and gives him an old car.

1936   Hiss joins the Trade Agreements division of the State Department as an aide to Assistant Secretary of State Francis B. Sayre.

1938   Chambers leaves the American Communist Party.

1939   In a private interview with Assistant Secretary of State Adolf Berle, Chambers says that Hiss and his brother Donald had been targeted by the Party as possible agents for the Soviet Union.

1941   The Hisses' only son, Tony, is born.

The United States enters World War II.

1944   Hiss, still a rising star in the State Department, is named deputy director of the Office of Special Political Affairs. The agency's responsibility is planning for a postwar world at peace. In August, Hiss organizes the

Dumbarton Oaks Conference, which lays the frame-work for the United Nations.

1945 As an aide to Secretary of State Edward R. Stettinius, Jr., Hiss is the American organizer for the Yalta confer-ence. In April, FDR dies. Hiss is promoted to the post of director of the State Department's Office of Political Affairs. He serves as secretary general of the San Fran-cisco Conference, which drafts the UN Charter.

1946 Hiss is interviewed for the first time by the FBI about the possibility of Communist connections.

1947 Hiss leaves the State Department to become president of the Carnegie Endowment for International Peace. His appointment is strongly supported by the future secretary of state John Foster Dulles, who is elected chairman of the Carnegie Endowment's board on the same day Hiss is named its president.

1948 Chambers testifies before the House Committee on Un-American Activities (HUAC) on August 3 that he and Hiss were both members of an underground Party group. He denies, however, that the group engaged in espionage.

Hiss testifies before HUAC and denies the charge that he was ever involved with the American Communist Party. He also denies having ever known Chambers. Most committee members want to drop the investiga-tion against Hiss, but California Representative Rich-ard M. Nixon persuades them to press on.

At a private meeting in the Commodore Hotel in New York, Hiss and Chambers confront each other before several HUAC members, including Nixon, and Hiss identifies Chambers as the man he once knew as George Crosley.

On August 25 Hiss and Chambers confront each other in a public hearing—the first congressional hearing ever televised. Two days later, when Chambers repeats his charges on *Meet the Press,* Hiss sues him for libel.

On November 4 Chambers testifies for the first time that he and Hiss *were* involved in espionage and that Hiss had passed on copies of State Department documents to him.

On December 2 Chambers leads two HUAC investigators to a garden patch on his Maryland farm, where he removes the top of a hollowed-out pumpkin and produces two strips of film and canisters containing three rolls of undeveloped film (two of which contained Navy Department documents). The "Pumpkin Papers" enter history.

On December 15 Hiss is indicted by a federal grand jury on two counts of perjury. The first count asserts that Hiss lied when he said he never saw Chambers after January 1937, and the second alleges that he lied when he said he never transmitted government documents to Chambers. Espionage charges are never filed against Hiss because the statute of limitations has expired. Significantly, the statute of limitations also applies to Chambers, who initially testified that his Communist group had *not* engaged in espionage. By the time Chambers testified in November, implicating Hiss and admitting to his own espionage, the statute had expired for both men.

1949　Hiss's first perjury trial ends in a hung jury.

1950　After a second trial Hiss is convicted on both counts of perjury.

1951　His appeals exhausted, Hiss goes to prison on March 22 to begin serving a five-year sentence.

1952 Chambers's autobiography, *Witness*, is published and becomes a bestseller.

Richard Nixon, largely on the strength of the national reputation he acquired as a result of his role in the HUAC investigation of Hiss, is selected as Dwight D. Eisenhower's running mate, and the Republican ticket is elected to the White House.

1954 Hiss is released from prison.

1957 Hiss's first book, *In the Court of Public Opinion*, is published. As in all of his subsequent statements, Hiss maintains his innocence.

1961 Whittaker Chambers dies.

1972 The "Hiss Act" is declared unconstitutional and Hiss's government pension is restored.

1975 Hiss, disbarred after his conviction, is readmitted to the Massachusetts bar by order of the state's Supreme Judicial Court.

1978 *Perjury*, a reexamination of the Hiss case by the historian Allen Weinstein, is published. Incorporating new materials released under the Freedom of Information Act, the book convinces many liberals who believed Hiss had been framed by the FBI that he was in fact guilty of perjury and that he had been a Communist spy.

1995 In July classified documents known as the Venona files are released at a ceremony attended by representatives of the CIA, the FBI, and the National Security Agency. The files consist of decoded messages from 1942 to 1946. One of the messages refers to a Soviet agent named "Ales," whom many scholars believe to have been Alger Hiss.

1996   Hiss dies on November 15 at age ninety-two. Before his death, he denies being "Ales."

1997–1999   A second edition of Weinstein's *Perjury*, published in 1997, makes use of the Venona files. The same year, Sam Tanenhaus publishes a massive biography, *Whittaker Chambers*, that is the first fully rounded portrait of Hiss's accuser. In 1999 *Venona: Decoding Soviet Espionage Operations in America*, by John Earl Haynes and Harvey Klehr, provides an even more extensive analysis of the Venona documents.

2007   Kai Bird, the Pulitzer Prize–winning coauthor of *American Prometheus: The Triumph and Tragedy of J. Robert Oppenheimer*, and Svetlana Chervonnaya, a Russian researcher, publish a seventeen thousand–word article in the *American Scholar* arguing that the Venona files show that Hiss could not have been "Ales," because he was in Washington when Ales's American control, quoted in Venona, placed Ales in Mexico. The real spy in the State Department, Bird and Chervonnaya argue, was Wilder Foote, another assistant to Secretary of State Stettinius at the time of the Yalta conference.

Tanenhaus, Whittaker Chambers's biographer, excoriates Bird and Chervonnaya's research in the *New Republic*.

To be continued, no doubt . . .

Notes

INTRODUCTION

1. Sam Tanenhaus, *Whittaker Chambers: A Biography* (New York, 1997), 301–303.
2. Alistair Cooke, *A Generation on Trial: The U.S.A. v. Alger Hiss* (New York, 1950), v.
3. Tanenhaus, *Whittaker Chambers*, 302.
4. Richard Nixon, *Six Crises* (Garden City, N.Y., 1962), 48.
5. Tanenhaus, *Whittaker Chambers*, 346; 417, from transcripts of first and second trials.
6. Allen Weinstein, *Perjury: The Hiss-Chambers Case* (New York, 1978), 548.
7. See Sam Tanenhaus, "The End of the Journey," *New Republic*, July 2, 2007.
8. Cooke, *A Generation on Trial*, 9.

ONE

Passions as Prologue

1. Richard Hofstadter, *Anti-Intellectualism in American Life* (New York, 1963), 40.

2. Diana Trilling, *The Beginning of the Journey* (New York, 1993), 180–181.

3. George H. Gallup, *The Gallup Poll: Public Opinion, 1935–1971* (New York, 1972), 1: 128.

4. George Gallup and Claude Robinson, "American Institute of Public Opinion-Surveys, 1935–38," *Public Opinion Quarterly* 2, no. 3 (1938): 388.

5. Gallup, *The Gallup Poll*, 1: 128–129.

6. Ibid., 1: 80.

7. Gallup and Robinson "American Institute of Public Opinion-Surveys," 389.

8. Cited in Thomas C. Reeves, *America's Bishop: The Life and Times of Fulton J. Sheen* (San Francisco, 2001), 102.

9. Cooke, *A Generation on Trial*, 3.

10. Quoted in Ronald Steel, *Walter Lippmann and the American Century* (Boston, 1980), 300.

11. Alger Hiss, *Recollections of a Life* (New York, 1988), 54–55, 59.

12. Quoted in G. Edward White, *Alger Hiss's Looking Glass Wars: The Covert Life of a Soviet Spy* (New York, 2004), 22.

13. Alger Hiss to Felix Frankfurter, December 13, 1929, Felix Frankfurter Papers, Library of Congress, quoted ibid., 22–23.

14. White, *Alger Hiss's Looking Glass Wars*, 25.

15. Hiss, *Recollections*, 61.

16. Tony Hiss, *Laughing Last* (Boston, 1977), 62.

17. Weinstein, *Perjury: The Hiss-Chambers Case* (New York, 1978), 98.

18. Hiss, *Recollections*, 62.

19. Quoted in Tanenhaus, *Whittaker Chambers*, 20.

20. Ibid., 28.

21. See Irving Howe and Lewis Coser, *The American Communist Party: A Critical History* (New York, 1974), 528.

22. Whittaker Chambers, *Witness* (New York, 1952), 207–208.

23. Hiss, *Recollections*, 14.

24. Chambers, *Witness*, 269.

25. Hiss, *Recollections*, 2.

26. Trilling, *The Beginning of the Journey*, 217–221.

27. Irving Howe, *A Margin of Hope* (New York, 1982), 61–89; Ir-

ving Kristol, "Memoirs of a Trotskyist," in *Reflections of a Neo-conservative* (New York, 1983), 4–13.

28. Howe, *A Margin of Hope*, 65.
29. Howe and Coser, *The American Communist Party*, 419.
30. Granville Hicks, "Communism and the American Intellectuals," in *Whose Revolution? A Study of the Future Course of Liberalism in the United States* (New York, 1941), 92.
31. Ibid., 93, 95.
32. Hiss, *Recollections*, 85.
33. Hicks, "Communism and the American Intellectuals," 97.
34. Hiss, *Recollections*, 96, 118, 125.
35. Ibid., 207.
36. Ibid., 208.
37. Ibid., 207–208.
38. Jeff Kisseloff, "Working for—and with—Alger Hiss," *The Alger Hiss Story: Search for the Truth*, http://homepages.nyu.edu/~th15/kisselof.html.
39. Chambers, *Witness*, 360–361.
40. Quoted in Tony Hiss, *The View from Alger's Window* (New York, 1999), 197.
41. Cooke, *A Generation on Trial*, 34–35.

T W O

The Eye of the Hurricane, 1948–1950

1. A. J. Liebling, "The Wayward Press: All About Inside-Policy Data," *New Yorker*, August 28, 1948.
2. Nixon, *Six Crises*, 5.
3. Tom Wicker, *One of Us: Richard Nixon and the American Dream* (New York, 1991), 54.
4. Richard Nixon, *The Memoirs of Richard Nixon* (New York, 1978), 55.
5. Gallup, *The Gallup Poll*, 2: 756–757, 771.
6. Quoted in Cooke, *A Generation on Trial*, 92.
7. Ibid., 97.
8. Robert Bendiner, "The Ordeal of Alger Hiss: Psychiatry, Law, and Politics," *Nation*, February 11, 1950.

9. Robert Bendiner, "The Trials of Alger Hiss," *Nation*, June 11, 1949.
10. "A Sinuous Trail Winds to a Close," *Chicago Daily Tribune*, January 22, 1950.
11. "After the Hiss Verdict," *Washington Post*, January 23, 1950.
12. "Mr. Hiss Found Guilty," *New York Times*, January 22, 1950.
13. Steen M. Johnson, "The Hiss Case Discussed," and John P. Frank, "Presumption of Innocence in Law," *New York Times*, Letters to the Editor, January 26, 1950.

THREE
Competing Narratives and Public Amnesia, 1950–1965

1. Gallup, *The Gallup Poll*, 2: 1114.
2. Chambers, *Witness*, 25.
3. Ibid., 16, 482.
4. Quoted in Hiss, *The View from Alger's Window*, 182.
5. Sidney Hook, "The Faiths of Whittaker Chambers," *New York Times Book Review*, May 25, 1952.
6. Alger Hiss, *In the Court of Public Opinion* (New York, 1957), 376.
7. Robert Bendiner, "The Ordeal of Alger Hiss, Part I," *Nation*, February 4, 1950.
8. White, *Alger Hiss's Looking-Glass Wars*, 121.
9. Arthur Miller, *Timebends* (New York, 1987), 342.
10. Brock Brower, "The Problems of Alger Hiss," *Esquire*, December 1960.
11. Ibid.
12. Ibid.
13. Chambers, *Witness*, 363.
14. Brower, "The Problems of Alger Hiss."

FOUR
The Best of Times, The Worst of Times, 1970–1980

1. Alger Hiss, "My Six Parallels," *New York Times*, July 23, 1973.
2. Jessica Mitford, *A Fine Old Conflict* (New York, 1977), 272.

3. White, *Alger Hiss's Looking-Glass Wars*, 140.
4. David Caute, *The Great Fear* (New York, 1978), 424.
5. Hiss, *Recollections*, 199.
6. Supreme Judicial Court for the Commonwealth (of Massachusetts), "Opinion on Reinstatement," August 5, 1975.
7. Thomas Moore, "Parting Shots," *Life*, April 7, 1972.
8. Victor Navasky, "The Case Not Proved Against Alger Hiss," *Nation*, April 8, 1978.
9. Quoted in Philip Nobile, "Allen Weinstein: Who Is He and What Has He Got on Alger Hiss?" *Politicks*, February 28, 1978.
10. Philip Nobile, "The State of the Art of Alger Hiss," *Harper's*, July 1976.
11. Weinstein, *Perjury*, 565.
12. Christopher Lehmann-Haupt, "Books of the Times," *New York Times*, April 7, 1978.
13. Ibid. See Navasky, "The Case Not Proved."
14. Interview with the author, March 29, 2006.

FIVE

The Rise of the Right and the Cold War at Twilight, 1980–1992

1. Ronald Reagan, "Remarks at Eureka College in Eureka, Illinois, February 6, 1984, http://www.presidency.ucsb.edu/ws/index.php?pid=39377&st=&st1=.
2. David Remnick, "Alger Hiss: Unforgiven and Unforgiving," *Washington Post Magazine*, October 12, 1986.
3. William Safire, "Begging for a Summit," *New York Times*, March 28, 1985.
4. Sidney Blumenthal, *The Rise of the Counter-Establishment: From Conservative Ideology to Political Power* (New York, 1986), 7.
5. Washington Post-ABC News Poll, December 6, 1987.
6. Saundra Saperstein Torry and John Mintz, "A Blasé Town Flips for Gorby," *Washington Post*, December 11, 1987.
7. Remnick, "Alger Hiss."

SIX

The Enemy Vanishes, 1992–2008

1. David Margolick, "After 40 Years, a Postscript on Hiss: Russian Official Calls Him Innocent," *New York Times*, October 29, 1992.
2. Tony Hiss, "My Father's Honor," *New Yorker*, December 16, 1992.
3. Serge Schmemann, "Russian General Retreats on Hiss," *New York Times*, December 17, 1992.
4. White, *Alger Hiss's Looking-Glass Wars*, 218.
5. "*In Re* Alger Hiss," *Nation*, November 16, 1992.
6. John Earl Haynes and Harvey Klehr, *Venona: Decoding Soviet Espionage in America* (New Haven, 1999), 171, 172.
7. Tanenhaus, "The End of the Journey."
8. Jeff Kisseloff, "Still Smearing Alger Hiss," *Counterpunch*, September 25, 2007, http://www.counterpunch.org/kisselof0925 2007.html.
9. Chambers, *Witness*, 472.
10. Alan Brinkley, "The New Deal and the Idea of the State," in *The Rise and Fall of the New Deal Order, 1930–1980*, ed. Steve Fraser and Gary Gerstle (Princeton, 1989), 92.

CONCLUSION

1. "Debating How Best to Love Your Country; Do You Fight Off Assaults on the System or Fight to Make the System Better?" *New York Times*, July 1, 2000.
2. Jacob Weisberg, "Cold War Without End," *New York Times Magazine*, November 28, 1999.
3. Quoted ibid.
4. Norman Podhoretz, *Breaking Ranks* (New York, 1979), 306.
5. John Podhoretz, interview with Deborah Solomon, *New York Times Magazine*, December 9, 2007.
6. Irving Kristol, *Reflections of a Neoconservative*, iv.
7. George Orwell, "James Burnham and the Managerial Revolution," *Polemic*, May 1946, http://www.netcharles.com/orwell/essays/james-burnham.htm.

8. Tanenhaus, "The End of the Journey."
9. Orwell, "James Burnham and the Managerial Revolution"; italics Orwell's.
10. In David Remnick, "Alger Hiss: Unforgiven and Unforgiving," *Washington Post Magazine*, October 12, 1986.

Selected Bibliography

Alter, Jonathan. *The Defining Moment: FDR's Hundred Days and the Triumph of Hope.* New York: Simon and Schuster, 2006.

Amalrik, Andrei. *Notes of a Revolutionary.* New York: Knopf, 1982.

Bernstein, Carl. *Loyalties: A Son's Memoir.* New York: Simon and Schuster, 1989.

Blumenthal, Sidney. *The Rise of the Counter-Establishment: From Conservative Ideology to Political Power.* New York: Times Books, 1986.

Brinkley, Alan. *The End of Reform: New Deal Liberalism in Recession and War.* New York: Knopf, 1995.

Caute, David. *The Great Fear.* New York: Simon and Schuster, 1978

Chambers, Whittaker. *Witness.* New York: Random House, 1952.

Cooke, Alistair. *A Generation on Trial: U.S.A. v. Alger Hiss.* New York: Knopf, 1950.

Coulter, Ann. *Treason: Liberal Treachery from the Cold War to the War on Terror.* New York: Crown Forum, 2003.

De Toledano, Ralph, and Victor Lasky. *Seeds of Treason: The True Story of the Hiss-Chambers Tragedy.* New York: Funk and Wagnalls, 1950.

Fraser, Steve, and Gary Gerstle, eds. *The Rise and Fall of the New Deal Order, 1930–1980.* Princeton: Princeton University Press, 1989.

Gallup, George H. *The Gallup Poll: Public Opinion, 1935–1971,* vols. 1–3. New York: Random House, 1972.

Gitlin, Todd. *The Sixties: Years of Hope, Days of Rage.* New York: Bantam, 1987.

Gorbachev, Mikhail. *Memoirs.* New York: Doubleday, 1995.

Griffith, Robert. *The Politics of Fear: Joseph R. McCarthy and the Senate.* Lexington: University Press of Kentucky, 1970.

Haynes, John Earl, and Harvey Klehr. *Venona: Decoding Soviet Espionage Operations in America.* New Haven: Yale University Press, 1999.

Hiss, Alger. *In the Court of Public Opinion.* New York: Knopf, 1957.

———. *Recollections of a Life.* New York: Seaver, 1988.

Hiss, Tony. *Laughing Last.* Boston: Houghton Mifflin, 1977.

———. *The View from Alger's Window.* New York: Knopf, 1999.

Hofstadter, Richard, *Anti-Intellectualism in American Life.* New York: Knopf, 1963.

Howe, Irving. *A Margin of Hope: An Intellectual Autobiography.* New York: Harcourt Brace Jovanovich, 1982.

Howe, Irving, and Lewis Coser. *The American Communist Party: A Critical History.* New York: Da Capo, 1974.

Isserman, Maurice. *If I Had a Hammer.* New York: Basic, 1987.

Jacoby, Susan. *Freethinkers: A History of American Secularism.* New York: Metropolitan, 2004.

Klehr, Harvey, John Earl Haynes, and Fridrikh Igorevich Firsov, Russian documents trans. Timothy D. Sergei. *The Secret World of American Communism*. New Haven: Yale University Press, 1995.

Kristol, Irving. *Reflections of a Neoconservative*. New York: Basic, 1983.

Miller, Arthur. *Timebends: A Life*. New York: Grove, 1987.

Mitford, Jessica. *A Fine Old Conflict*. New York: Knopf, 1977.

Navasky, Victor. *Naming Names*. New York: Viking, 1980.

Nixon, Richard. *The Memoirs of Richard Nixon*. New York: Grosset and Dunlap, 1978.

———. *Six Crises*. New York: Doubleday, 1962.

Podhoretz, Norman. *Breaking Ranks*. New York: Harper and Row, 1979.

Radosh, Ronald, and Joyce Milton. *The Rosenberg File: A Search for the Truth*. New York: Holt, Rinehart, and Winston, 1983.

Reeves, Thomas C. *America's Bishop: The Life and Times of Fulton J. Sheen*. San Francisco, 2001.

Remnick, David. *Lenin's Tomb*. New York: Random House, 1993.

Schlesinger, Arthur, Jr. *The Crisis of the Old Order, 1919–1933*. Boston: Houghton Mifflin. 1957.

Schrecker, Ellen W. *No Ivory Tower: McCarthyism and the Universities*. New York: Oxford University Press, 1986.

Smith, John Chabot. *Alger Hiss: The True Story*. New York: Penguin, 1977.

Talmadge, Irving DeWitt, ed. *Whose Revolution? A Study of the Future Course of Liberalism in the United States*. New York: Howell, Soskin, 1941.

Tanenhaus, Sam. *Whittaker Chambers: A Biography*. New York: Random House, 1997.

Trilling, Diana. *The Beginning of the Journey*. New York: Harcourt Brace, 1991.

Trilling, Lionel. *The Liberal Imagination*. New York: Viking, 1950.

———. *The Middle of the Journey*. New York: Scribner's, 1975.

Weinstein, Allen. *Perjury: The Hiss-Chambers Case*. New York: Knopf, 1978.

Weinstein, Allen, and Alexander Vassiliev. *The Haunted Wood: Soviet Espionage in America — The Stalin Era*. New York: Random House, 1999.

White, G. Edward. *Alger Hiss's Looking-Glass Wars: The Covert Life of a Soviet Spy*. New York: Oxford University Press, 2004.

Wicker, Tom. *One of Us: Richard Nixon and the American Dream*. New York: Random House, 1991.

Zeligs, Meyer. *Friendship and Fratricide: An Analysis of Whittaker Chambers and Alger Hiss*. New York: Viking, 1967.

Acknowledgments

This book, like most of my books, was written in the Frederick Lewis Allen Room of the New York Public Library—which is, as far as I am concerned, the greatest institution in the great city where I live. I owe special thanks to David Smith, a senior research librarian who, among many other duties, presides over the sometimes unruly stable of nonfiction writers who work in the Allen Room. Three of my fellow Allen Room denizens, Mark Lee, Mark Lamster, and Alex Rose, provided encouragement and a good laugh when they were most needed.

Jonathan Brent, editorial director of the Yale University Press, provided invaluable counsel along the way, and Sarah Miller presided over preparation of the manuscript for the final stages of the editing process. My special thanks go to Dan Heaton for his meticulous copyediting and spirited commentary.

Finally, as always, I wish to thank my agents, Georges and Anne Borchardt, for thirty-five years of friendship and the best representation an author could want.

Index